Every Lady Deserves a Chance

The Story of the Walter Hoving Home

John Benton

“Praise the Lord for the Christian ministry of John and Elsie Benton of the Walter Hoving Home. Elsie and John are a veritable beacon light of Christian love, beaming warm understanding, healing, and transforming Christian Holy spirit power in countless lives of desperate young women who have lost their way. God bless you beautiful Bentons!”

— DALE EVANS ROGERS

“Never before have so many young people in our country become so disenchanted, so bored and burdened with life, that they fall easy prey to the various escapes being offered. They find out too late that escapes such as drugs, turn instead into traps from which few escape.

The Walter Hoving Home ... is a place where such a girl can find a warm, loving welcome; receive solid, practical help, and most important of all, be introduced to the Lord Jesus Christ Who alone can forgive sins, give power to resist temptation and make life worth living.”

— RUTH GRAHAM

“In my visits to the Walter Hoving Home . . . I’ve literally seen Jesus in action.

Year after year, girls with no hope and tragic pasts are literally swept off the dead end street . . . and given new lives and new personalities. They are nursed to health, given whole new visions of life and their own worth, and introduced to Jesus. The transformations are miraculous, and I’m grateful for the chance to participate in the on-going miracles at the Walter Hoving Home.”

— **Pat Boone**

I have seen the Walter Hoving Home ministry first hand and I am an enthusiastic supporter. It is a good example of people of the Church obeying our Lord’s command to reach out to those in need.”

— **Charles W. Colson, Founder/Chairman Prison Fellowship**

CONTENTS

Introduction

When Elsie and I get up every morning, we never know what to expect in our ministry. Sometimes it can be life threatening; then there are temptations that could destroy us or pressures that could drive a person crazy. But in the end, God has always — and I mean *always* — come through for us.

As I prepared to write a second book about the ministry, I began to remember many things that I had not included in the first book, *One Lady At A Time*. In the following pages, you will read more about what really goes on inside the Walter Hoving Home, as well as what goes on inside of me!

I will share with you my temptations, fears and frustration; but most of all; I will share how God has come through every time, even in my most desperate hours. I hope this book will not only give you a deeper insight into the ministry of the Walter Hoving Home, but will also inspire a faith in you to believe and trust in God like you have never believed in Him before.

CHAPTER 1

WANNA MEET THE MAFIA?

After another very long and trying day, I plopped myself into bed. Sleep, though, never came easily.

I had just come back from the streets. Even today, after all these years, we still go out in the city streets, spreading the gospel of love, letting the ladies of the night know that Christ can set them free.

That evening I had been up in Times Square, where many ladies were prostituting to support their drug habits. As I stood at the corner of Forty-Eighth and Broadway, a girl walked toward me.

I immediately went up to her and gave her some literature about our home. When I identified myself and told her who I was and where I was from, I noticed that she kept glancing over my shoulder. Still, she was gracious, took my literature and walked on down the street.

After I had the chance to talk to some other ladies, I decided to get a quick cup of coffee. I stepped into a coffee shop, got my cup of coffee and walked back outside. A woman approached me. "What are you giving out to those ladies?" she asked.

I looked at the woman carefully. She was probably around fifty years old. She didn't look like a prostitute; yet, she did not look like a cop either. Who was she?

While explaining to her who I was and what I was doing, a girl came up to us. The woman turned and said to the girl, "Go across the street and stand on that corner over there."

Looking very frightened, the girl quickly obeyed and went across the street. As soon as the girl was gone, the woman said, "Can I see some of the stuff you're handing out?"

Something made me nervous about this woman. What was she trying to get at? I gave her some literature. She looked it over and asked, "A re-hab program for women who are on drugs?"

"We are a Christian organization," I replied.

As we were talking, another girl walked up to the woman. They stepped aside and had a private conversation. I could not hear what was going on. As, the girl turned back toward me, I found myself looking into another frightened face.

Walking back to where I was standing the woman said, "Can I keep this literature?"

"Sure," I answered, "That's why we're out here."

With that the woman abruptly walked away.

I stood there thinking about what had just happened and it hit me. This woman was a Madam, and these prostitutes were working for her.

Fortunately, this Madam did not cause me any trouble. Madams are the equivalent of a man pimp, and I understand they can get just as vicious. Thank God, nothing happened.

I continued to witness for a while and then headed back home.

It was after midnight, when I fell into bed and finally dozed off. Sometime later, the phone rang, startling me. Quickly I reached over and grabbed it.

"Hello," I said.

A woman's voice on the other end asked, "Are you the man who was up in Times Square this evening?" I thought it was one of those ladies calling for help. "Yes, I am. Can I help you?"

"Were you talking with a woman?" she asked.

"In fact, I talked to a number of ladies" I said. "Were you one of them?"

I felt that she was playing a cat and mouse game with me and I really wanted to go back to sleep.

"Ma'am, I'm here to help you," I said. "How can I help you?"

Then she asked abruptly, "Were you talking to a woman outside a coffee shop?"

"Yes, that was me," I said.

"I would like to talk to you," she said sternly.

I grumbled to myself and said, "I'd be happy to talk to you. I'll be in my office tomorrow, you can come and see me then."

"I need to talk to you now, I mean right now," she replied, and then paused. I felt kind of guilty. Maybe I shouldn't be so abrupt.

She said, "You actually were talking to my sister, and we'd like to talk to you."

"I'd be more than happy to meet with you," I said.

The woman said, "If it is not too much of an inconvenience, we'd like for you to come over here to Times Square and meet us in this restaurant."

"Now?" I asked.

"Yes. This is something very serious. We want to talk to you now."

My heart started racing. This whole evening with this woman had been so strange. I'd just assumed that she was a Madam. But what was this all about?

The woman said, "Here's the address. When you get there, walk straight through the restaurant and into the back room. We'll be sitting there at a round table. If someone stops you and asks you what you're doing, just tell them that someone is going to meet you at the back table. Okay?"

I guess I was half asleep or something because I quickly agreed, "Okay, I'll be there."

The woman then said, "Whatever you do, do not tell anybody, and I mean *anybody*, where you are going, who you are going to see, or anything about this."

My heart beat even faster. Was this a set up? I guess it was my sleepiness, stupidity, ignorance, or something like that, which had me saying, "I'll see you in about half an hour."

I looked over at Elsie. She was sound asleep. Elsie is one of those people who puts her head on the pillow and is out like a light. I wish I could do that.

I slid out of bed and got dressed.

At that time, our ministry was in Brooklyn. As I was driving across the Brooklyn Bridge, it suddenly hit me, "What in the world am I doing? If it's a set up and I get killed, nobody knows where I am. This is really stupid."

I told myself that I was not going to go through with this one. I was going to get to the end of the bridge, turn around and head back home. No sirree, I was not going to be that stupid. I still wanted to live and reach some more of these ladies.

When I got to the end of the Brooklyn Bridge, I can only say that something came over me and that still, small voice that I have come to recognize through the years said, "Meet with the ladies."

I shrugged my shoulders, and in my spirit, I told God that I hoped He wasn't making a mistake. Something just didn't feel right about all this.

I got to Times Square and found the restaurant.

They say New York City never sleeps. It's true. Twenty-four hours a day, seven days a week, you'll always find activity on the streets.

As I walked into the restaurant and started towards the back, a man stopped me. "Can I help you?" he asked.

"I'm supposed to meet two ladies in the back room," I replied.

"Yes, they're waiting for you. It's back

there," he said, pointing to the rear of the restaurant.

I walked into the back room, and there sitting at a round table were two ladies. I recognized the first one right away. She was the one I had talked to.

The other woman was something else. She oozed wealth; she was wearing this big, beautiful fur coat and displayed huge diamonds on her fingers.

The lady I had met earlier said, "Please sit down; this is my sister. She wants to talk to you."

I sat down and the sister looked at me and said, "Frances tells me you spoke with her tonight."

Glancing over the sister's shoulder, I saw a menacing looking man standing there, just glaring at me.

And then it hit me. I'm right in the middle of the Mafia, and this is a crime syndicate. They were involved in prostitution, and here I was meeting with the Mafia. My heart slammed into my throat. How would I get out of this one?

I couldn't believe I'd been so stupid. I should have told Elsie where I was going.

What could I do now? The woman sensed my anxiety. She reached out and put her hand on my arm. "Relax. Just relax. Nothing is going to happen to you."

Somehow, I did not believe her. I supposed that was what the Mafia told everybody right before they iced them.

Quickly, but thoroughly, I explained what our ministry does. If they were going to kill me, I was going to give my best shot at witnessing to these ladies.

I began to tell them about Jesus and about the gospel and how He could change lives. Much to my amazement, they just sat there listening.

In fact, the well-dressed woman leaned forward, as though she were hanging onto every word. All this time, the other gal, Frances, whom I had talked to on the street earlier, did not say a word.

Then her sister asked, "Can you help Frances?"

"That's why God sent us into this ministry, to help someone like Frances," I replied.

The woman said, "Frances has got a drug habit, and we as a family cannot handle it any longer." Then she asked, "Can I get you something to eat?"

Actually that wouldn't have been such a bad idea. I suddenly realized how hungry I was. But I really wanted to get out of there, even though the Mafia was being kind and nice, I knew that they could get mean and ugly.

"I really need to get back. I've got a long day ahead of me," I said and promptly stood up.

"Well, we want Frances to go with you. We're hoping you can help her with your program," the woman said. Frances stood up. I shook hands with the woman, and Frances and I headed out the door.

When we hit the street, I breathed a great sigh of relief. Thank God I was still alive.

As Frances and I headed back to the center, I asked her how she got on drugs. She said, "I need to really tell you what's happened to me."

"Sure go ahead," I said.

Frances began to cry as she told me her story. She said she had gotten involved in sexual immorality. She didn't tell me she was a Madam, but I knew that was her job.

Frances told me that she had gotten into drugs and couldn't shake the habit. And then, the drugs led to a life of sexual perversion.

Frances began to explain to me that she was having sex with other women, but then it became more perverted, and during the sexual encounters, she and her partner would beat each other with coat hangers.

It was very sadistic, and she couldn't get out of it.

Elsie and I were new to the ministry, and I didn't know much about this problem of homosexuality.

Then Frances said, "I haven't taken a bath in days. I'm filthy. I'm so dirty and mixed up in my mind that I no longer feel like a human being."

"Well, Frances, you've come to the right place. Christ is going to change all that." I responded.

When we got back to the home, Frances wanted to take a shower. I was able to get some towels, and find an empty bed for her. I woke up one of the girls for some assistance and told her I had just gotten Frances off the street.

I said good night to Frances, and went back to bed.

This time, sleep was not to come. As I lay there, I could tell that Elsie never even knew I had been gone. Bless her dear soul, she was still sound asleep!

At that time, we had an old house, which had actually once been the home of the Mayor of Brooklyn. A lot of the bedrooms had their own little sinks in them. I don't know what happened, but I found myself at the sink in our bedroom washing my hands. It occurred to me that it was the third time that night.

As I stood there washing my hands, I began thinking about the terrible perversion that Frances had gotten herself into. Images of filth and animalistic, sadistic behavior appeared before me.

Exhausted from my thoughts and the events of the evening, I began to plead for the blood of Jesus to cleanse my mind from that filth. Looking back, I felt so wretched thinking about that type of life.

Finally, I crawled back into bed and just lay there. The next thing I recall was the alarm clock screaming at me.

I dragged my tired bones out of bed. Elsie was already up. I told her what had happened. She could not believe all I had been through while she slept.

I tried to convince her it wasn't a dream, and that she would meet Frances.

We were able to present Christ to Frances while she was with us. Even though she did not complete the full program, I do know that she left knowing that there was a better way to live.

It was through Christ.

However, that was not the last time I got involved with the Mafia.

It was in a section of Brooklyn, which we

often frequented to talk to the ladies, that I encountered an Italian, Mafia type, a little girl named Cecilia. Mean and ornery, when I'd give her a tract, she would cuss me out, tear it up and throw it at my feet.

But, I would not give up on her. Every time I saw her, I'd give her another one, and sure enough, she'd cuss me out and tear it up.

One night, I couldn't take any more.

After Cecilia once again tore up the tract, she turned and walked away. Some angry force welled up in me, and I felt this power surging in my right leg. I was about to kick her in the seat of her pants.

No woman was going to do that to God's literature!

Some people might call it righteous indignation. I certainly don't think it was the Spirit of God moving me at that particular moment. It must have been the spirit of the devil.

Finally I took control of my leg, gritted my teeth and walked away. I vowed never to approach her again, and I didn't.

Then one day right out of the blue, Cecilia showed up on our front door step. She wanted help and, of course, we took her in.

A few weeks after Cecilia had been with us, I told her how a pimp in the area kept giving me a hard time. Cecilia said, "Just say the word."

"Just say the word? What do you mean by that?" I asked.

She smiled cryptically and repeated, "Just say the word."

I still couldn't figure it out. Again, I asked Cecilia, "What do you mean, just say what word?"

She said, "Just tell me, I'll call my family, and trust me, you'll never hear from that pimp again."

Suddenly it dawned on me. I knew what she was getting at. Her family was Mafia! All I had to do was say the word, she would call them, and they would kill that pimp.

I said, "Cecilia, you're a Christian now. That's not the way we handle things." "Oh, yeah," she said, "That's how we used to do it."

Then I explained to Cecilia what it means to give your life to Christ, and let the Lord fight your battles. She seemed satisfied with that, and later came to know Christ in a real way.

I often think about that incident. When I met Frances in Times Square, I had thought the Mafia was after me. Later, because of my connection with Cecilia, the Mafia would have done away with one of *my* enemies.

Of course, that's the way God does things — which makes me feel rather smug knowing that even the Mafia can become a friend in times of great need.

As we continued to develop the ministry, there were many other dangers we had to face. At one time, four young men were coming to kill me. They were armed, and it was one of the scariest moments of my life. More about that, later...

CHAPTER 2

The World's Greatest Con Artist

Shortly after we arrived in New York in 1965, David Wilkerson, the author of *The Cross and the Switch Blade* and founder of Teen Challenge, invited Elsie and me to join his staff. Dave needed a crusade director and someone to take over the women's ministry of Teen Challenge. He asked us to do it, and we did.

In New York, we never seemed to have enough space. In fact, Dave and I shared his office. Both of our desks were jammed into the same room. One day I was sitting at my desk, doing some work on a crusade. Dave was working at his desk as well.

All of a sudden, a lady, about thirty years old, burst through the door, screaming at the top of her voice, "Help me! Help me! Help me! Help me!"

Wild eyed, she ran towards Dave's desk. My mouth fell open. I didn't know what was going to happen next.

This girl again screamed, "Help me! Help me! Help me! Help me!"

I looked at Dave. He was sitting calmly at his desk, pen in hand, writing something on a piece of paper, not reacting at all.

Looking over at me with bleary, hysterical eyes she yelled again, "Help me! Help me! Help me! Help me!"

I stood up and looked bewilderedly at Dave. The girl then fell to her knees in front of his desk, her arms raised, and said, "Please Mr. Wilkerson! Please Mr. Wilkerson!"

Would you believe, Dave didn't pay one bit of attention to her, and just kept writing on this piece of paper? It was as if he was stone deaf.

Getting no response from Dave, the girl fell onto her knees and came hobbling over to me. She was about to reach up and grab me, when Dave yelled, "Iris! Get up and sit down!"

To my amazement, she got up and sat down in a chair in front of Dave. Dave said, "I told you this would happen. You wouldn't believe me, but I knew this was going to happen."

Later on, Dave told me the story. Iris was a successful con artist with a drug habit. She had discovered many ways of conning people and organizations to support her drug habit. Her most recent con game involved a White Castle Restaurant. White Castles are these small hamburger places in New York that are quite famous.

Iris had gone into a White Castle to get a burger. She was standing there eating her hamburger when a guy walked up to her and said, "These are wonderful hamburgers. I'd like to buy one of these places."

Iris could tell this was a man from a foreign country, who probably had money and was naive about America. Iris's brain went into motion, and she came up with a scheme.

Iris said to this man, "Now, isn't that something. I happen to own this restaurant, and I'm planning to sell it."

"Really?" the man asked.

"Yes, but I have got to tell you something, sir," Iris said, "My husband and I are getting a divorce, and I don't want anyone to know that I'm selling it."

The man said, "Well give me a good deal, and I'll pay cash."

Iris sprang into action. She grabbed the guy by the arm, took him outside and whispered, "I'm desperate to get rid of this place. My husband and I are about ready to kill each other. I just want to sell it for quick cash and get away from him."

"Name your price," the man said.

"Fifty thousand dollars, cash," Iris replied.

The man said, "I don't have the money with me, but I'll get it for you tomorrow." Iris then said, "Here, come let me take you on a quick trip through the restaurant, so you'll really see what you're getting." Iris knew that in the con game, you always want to come up with different ways to reinforce what you are trying to do. She knew this tour would do that.

Of course, you may be thinking that would be a crazy thing to do, certainly, somewhere along the way, he would discover her deceit. But, with the confidence of experience, Iris knew differently.

She took the guy, and as she walked through the place, Iris would smile at different people and say, "Hi, how are you? Hi, how are you?"

And, of course, when you ask how people are, they generally answer. It's a natural response; even in New York City.

Would you believe, Iris took this guy all through that restaurant, smiling and greeting people, and then they walked out the back door.

Iris said to the man, "Now, this is the deal. You have got to promise me that you won't tell anyone that I am selling the place to you for cash. If my husband finds out, the deal is off. And, sir, trust me, you will never find a better deal than this. But, so help me, if you utter one word to anybody of what you are doing, the deal is off, okay?"

The man said, "Trust me, I will not utter one word to anybody, not one word."

Iris said, "Now, tomorrow at ten o'clock in the morning, I want you to come with your cash. I'll have my lawyer with me, we'll sign the necessary papers and the deal will be done."

"Tomorrow, I'll be here at ten o'clock sharp with fifty thousand dollars," the man said and walked off. Iris walked off the other way.

Iris went to a dime store and purchased some legal papers that looked very official. She got a friend of hers to dress in a black suit and carry a brief case, and the following day they met the potential buyer.

Iris introduced her friend as her lawyer. They signed the papers, and the unsuspecting gentleman handed Iris fifty thousand dollars in cash.

The new owner of White Castle restaurant took the papers, said, "Thank you," and started to walk inside.

He turned to Iris and said, "The first thing I'm going to do is let some of those people go. You've got too many people working here."

As he headed toward the door, Iris and her friend quickly disappeared out of sight. With fifty thousand dollars, Iris had succeeded at another con game. She gave her friend some of the money, and proceeded to her favorite drug dealer. It was time to celebrate.

After getting high, Iris felt remorseful and knew that this was not the way she should live her life. She had heard about Teen Challenge and checked herself in.

Iris then told Dave about how she'd got the money and wanted to give the balance of the money to Dave. Dave didn't want to get involved in something like that and told her she would have to go to the restaurant and try to find the guy, give him the money back and face the consequences.

Of course, Iris wouldn't hear of it. She didn't want to risk going to jail. Dave said he would recommend some mission organizations that she could donate the money to. She whipped around and stomped out of Dave's office.

Dave called out to her, "If you don't do as I say, that money will curse you and it will destroy your life!"

And now, here we were, a few months later, with Iris bursting through the door, screaming for help.

Dave calmed Iris down, and we took her into the girls' home. So help me, I have never met such an unusual person as Iris. She started serving the Lord and began telling Elsie and me all about her past as a con artist.

She would go into hotels and look for carpeting that was frayed and coming apart. Then as she was walking around, she would supposedly trip on the carpet, grab her leg and start screaming out in pain. The hotel manager would come over, Iris would point to the torn carpet and scream that she was going to sue them.

Of course, this was negligence on the part of the manager, not having the carpet repaired, and the manager knew that he was in deep trouble. Iris would then work out a deal with the manager, get paid off and go on her way.

She would look for broken cement on sidewalks. In taxicabs, if the seat was not right or something, when the cab stopped she would fall out and pretend to be injured.

Iris was always looking for the easy money, always looking for a way to con somebody, and she was very, very successful at it.

Unfortunately, Iris didn't stay long at the ministry with us. She left and went back to her world of drugs and con artistry.

The last I heard she had died of a drug overdose.

Elsie and I had tried our best to help Iris, and we came pretty close to succeeding. But unfortunately, the power of sin had her firmly in its clutches. She just couldn't overcome its tenacious grip, couldn't trust the power of Jesus to completely set her free.

The loss of Iris hurt us deeply, as it does with anyone we lose. But still, we keep trying to help more ladies, and thank God, more and more of them are making it through and today are serving the Lord.

Our place in Brooklyn was really crowded, and we knew that we had to have larger facilities. And, through a miracle of God, we got our current home. In my previous book *One Lady At A Time* I told the story in greater detail about how we were able to purchase our twenty-three acre estate in Garrison, New York.

As I explained earlier, it was through my meeting with Walter Hoving, the Chairman of Tiffany's, and the Alton Jones Foundation, that God blessed us with this beautiful place.

When we moved out of Brooklyn and up

to Garrison, New York, we called the home *The Walter Hoving Home* in honor of Mr. Hoving. He was the one who made it possible to get the money to purchase the estate.

We moved to Garrison in 1967. Even so, I did not relinquish my responsibilities at the Brooklyn Teen Challenge. I was the Associate Director, and in addition to being Crusade Director, I had many other responsibilities in Brooklyn.

Back then, our whole lives were focused on the ministry. We worked around the clock, twenty-four hours a day, seven days a week, week after week, and never took a day off.

Eventually that rigorous schedule took a severe toll on my life, and I came very close to an extreme nervous breakdown. Later on, I'll tell you how the Lord got me through that one.

Meanwhile, we kept going out on the streets, still making contact with ladies in trouble.

Elsie and I have three children. One time, when our children were quite young, our son Jim was talking to one of the neighbor boys up in Garrison. One of the ladies overheard the boy ask Jim what his father did. Jim innocently replied, "My daddy brings home a different lady every night."

Of course, what Jim really meant was that when I came up to Garrison from Brooklyn, I often brought ladies with me to come into the program. That was part of the ministry.

I still get a laugh whenever I imagine that boy's parents reacting to the news that the guy who lived next door brought home different ladies every night.

There were five different places in New York City that I would routinely go to look for ladies to bring into the ministry. As we developed friendships with the ladies, they would call us.

By this time, we'd been able to build a new office building for Teen Challenge. One afternoon as I sat in my office in Brooklyn, I received a call from a lady named Andrea. Elsie and I knew her from the streets. She was such a nice girl that she'd found a special place in our hearts.

I told Andrea I would come pick her up and take her to Garrison. But when she stumbled into my car, I immediately realized that she was high. We prefer to not take ladies into the shelter when they are high, but sometimes we have to.

As we were traveling on the Saw Mill Parkway, on the way up to Garrison. Andrea kept talking, and I tried to make the conversation as interesting as possible.

I asked her how she was doing physically.

She said that she had a bunch of abscesses and that they were infected. (This comes from using a dirty needle, and is quite common).

She said, "I have a big one here, on my hip. Here I'll show it to you." She raised her hip and started pulling down her slacks and panties.

I quickly yelled, "No, Andrea, I believe you. Keep your pants up."

I could just imagine some guy driving by and seeing this girl taking off her pants in my car. Suppose it was a preacher friend of mine who saw all this? I probably could have lost my papers, lost my ministry, lost my wife, lost my kids and everything else.

But, thank God, Andrea pulled up her trousers, and to this day, I have never seen an abscessed hip on any lady.

As we arrived at Garrison, I was driving into the parking lot. We were right by the main entrance and I asked Andrea if she had any drugs on her.

Much to my shock, she grabbed her sweater, pulled it up, and exposed her bare breasts. I quickly said, "Okay, okay, I believe you! I believe you!"

It wasn't enough that she had already

pulled her pants down; now she was flashing her bare breasts at me.

Then she pulled her sweater down and kind of adjusted it a little bit.

My heart was beating like crazy. I immediately looked up to the second floor to see if anybody was watching us. If they were, I can only imagine what they were thinking.

I never did hear anything about it, so I guess it was okay.

Sometimes I am asked, "How do I survive as a man in this ministry with these ladies, many of whom have been prostitutes, seducing men?"

I must admit that I am a red blooded American man, and like many men, I certainly have passions. At times, temptation has tried to seize me, but thank God, to this day, I have never crossed that line of immorality. It has not been easy though.

For thirty years I have been accused of many different things. In fact, when I first got to Teen Challenge, one of the ladies accused me of having sex with her. That really made me very, very angry. Not only the fact that I supposedly had sex with her, but also that the girl who accused me weighed about three hundred and fifty pounds, with tattoos all over her body, and no teeth!

When this accusation came up, I told Elsie that if I was going to go "over the hill," I wanted to make sure it was with Miss America, because no matter who you get involved with, you're still going to burn, and you had better make it worthwhile. (Of course, I hope you know that I'm just kidding!)

I would never jeopardize this ministry, or compromise my relationship with my wonderful wife over a few moments of temptation.

I was accused by a girl, who had come to us from South Carolina, of fathering her child. In fact, she had a baby boy and named him John, after me. Can you imagine someone intentionally lying like that? Maybe you too have been wrongly accused before.

Let me give you some advice as to how we should respond when we are falsely accused.

My position is that the Lord knows my heart, and the Lord knows that I have kept myself clean.

If any of these kinds of accusations, or furthermore, any other type of accusations come up against me, I just say in my heart, "It's their problem, not mine."

A dear minister friend of mine gave me some advice years ago when I was criticized as director of a youth camp. He told me that he takes the criticism, looks at it, and if it is not true, he throws it over his shoulder and keeps marching right on.

Well, thank God, I just keep marching on.

As the ministry continued to grow in Garrison, we kept facing obstacles that were almost impossible to overcome. This is especially true when you pour your heart and soul into a lady and think that she has finally made it. Then all of a sudden you hear the worst possible news.

I want to tell you about Cindy.

CHAPTER 3

LADIES' GREAT FAITH

I just wish I had the faith of our ladies. It is unbelievable that after all they have been through, enduring the worst possible degradations imaginable in our great society; they can still trust God and get answers.

They keep teaching me great lessons of faith.

Like Cindy.

Cindy came from the State of Pennsylvania, and was from a very good family. After Cindy got out of high school, her parents sent her to college. She was a very diligent girl.

She got a job with the state government, and became a supervisor in the welfare department. Her responsibility was issuing checks to welfare recipients.

Cindy was a very gracious person; she would even cash the checks for welfare recipients, and of course, get the money to them. But then a tragic thing happened.

Cindy met this guy and she thought that she was really in love.

But there was a problem. He was a drug addict, hooked on heroin. And, as usually happens in such cases, it wasn't long until Cindy became a heroin addict herself, plunging into a negative cycle of co-dependency.

Her habit quickly took over her life, getting bigger, and bigger, and bigger.

Along with the big habit, came the eternal problem of the junkie. How do you get enough money to keep buying dope?

Then Cindy got a bright idea. This is the plan that she developed.

In her work as a supervisor, she issued checks to welfare recipients. Cindy decided she would issue checks to fictitious names, cash the checks and put the money in her pocket.

Of course, it didn't stay in her pocket long. She took the money and bought heroin to support her habit.

Finally, inevitably, she got caught. Cindy realized she had made a terrible mistake, and broken the law. Because her habit was so bad, the police had to take her to the hospital, and under constant twenty-four hour guard, she kicked her dope habit.

Then, somebody told her about the

Walter Hoving Home. The court allowed Cindy to come here into the program. Cindy did just great. Elsie and I really loved her. She was one of the best ladies we ever had in the program. And, thank God, Cindy did graduate. She had a desire to serve the Lord and went on to Bible school.

Then, after that, some severe problems developed.

Cindy was supposed to go back to court to be sentenced for the crime she had committed. I spoke with her lawyer in Philadelphia, who had kept contact with her while she was going through the program.

I told him that Elsie and I would be happy to go down and appear in court to testify on her behalf. Sometimes we do this, and the judges are very lenient.

The lawyer told me there certainly wouldn't be a problem with this one, with the progress that Cindy had made. Also, since this was her first offense, it was pretty well cut and dry. She would almost certainly receive a suspended sentence.

Cindy went down to the court. As she stood before the judge, she felt confident that things were going to turn out all right. At least, that's what her lawyer had reassured her over and over again.

But then, the worst thing happened.

The judge decided to make an example of Cindy's case. He said that he had no alternative but to sentence her for two to ten years in the state penitentiary.

The lawyer called me immediately. When he told me what happened, it seemed that my whole world had fallen apart.

Furthermore, how could God, who seemed to always be just and merciful, allow this to happen? I just couldn't believe it.

Cindy was sent to the state penitentiary in Pennsylvania.

Elsie and I tried to see her as soon as we could, unfortunately we had to be cleared. It took three months for the clearance to come through. We finally made arrangements to drive down there, which took about six hours.

All the way down during that long drive, I kept trying to figure out what I was going to say to Cindy. Could I just blurt out, "This is God's will."

Are you kidding?

No, I could not, because I knew that after the visit, Elsie and I would be leaving the prison, but Cindy would still be there, facing her ten years. No, I really couldn't say that.

But what could I say?

I finally memorized a good speech. Its substance was simple, just believe in God, no matter what. I didn't know if those words of encouragement would be enough for Cindy, but at least I would try.

When we got to the penitentiary we went through the clearance procedures and ended up in the visiting area. As we sat in the waiting room, I watched the clock and the door where Cindy was to come from.

A whole hour went by. No Cindy.

I knew what had happened. Cindy undoubtedly had become bitter over this court decision to place her in the state penitentiary. There she was in Bible school, preparing herself for ministry, and this is what God did to her.

Thinking about that, I could understand her bitterness.

Still, Elsie and I waited. We waited another hour. I knew that there was no way that Cindy was going to come and meet us.

I went up to one of the officers, and told them that I had been waiting two hours. She told me that sometimes it takes awhile for them to get cleared and come to the visiting area. She suggested that I should wait longer.

I wanted to tell her the circumstances surrounding Cindy, especially about her bitterness towards God. But Elsie and I decided to wait just a little longer.

We were sitting at this table looking across the waiting area, when Cindy came through the door.

Elsie and I immediately jumped up and walked to the center of the room where Cindy met us. As I looked into Cindy's eyes, I was going to blurt out my memorized speech, but so help me, my mind went completely blank.

A lump stuck in my throat, and I couldn't say a word. Then I used a tactic I had learned from some of the women.

When you don't know what to do, start to cry. You'd be amazed what tears can do, so I started to cry. I tried again to say something, but nothing would come out.

Elsie and I both hugged Cindy. I don't know what it was, but the emotion was so strong that I couldn't even speak. Finally, after a couple of deep breaths, I mumbled, "Cindy, how is it?"

To this day, I will never — I mean never — forget Cindy's words.

Cindy said, "Dad, I'm in prison, but the prison is not in me."

Then I really began to cry. This time not tears of resentment or even confusion, but tears of joy. Cindy had found that place in God's Will that would not allow the circumstances to destroy her.

She went on to say, "And would you believe, because of my Bible school education, the Chaplain has let me preach on Sunday mornings, and the chapel is packed!"

I just wish you could have seen the big, broad smile on Cindy's face.

Here she was a preacher in one of the greatest mission fields in the world, the state penitentiary.

We sat down and talked for quite a while. Cindy said that she knew that whatever had happened to her was God's will, and that she had no bitterness whatsoever.

God knew what he was doing all along. By condemning her to this temporary state of purgatory, which He knew she could master, He was bringing salvation to those who needed it most.

As I sat there listening to Cindy, I was really embarrassed by my own lack of faith. Cindy taught me a great lesson. And fortunately, that is not the end of this story.

Cindy was such a model prisoner and an encouragement to the other prisoners, as well as to the staff. As a result, the staff actually wrote up a petition asking the judge to reconsider her sentence.

A miracle happened.

Nine months later, Cindy was paroled.

Today, she is a great, strong Christian woman and married, with two children. She works as the bookkeeper for a bus company.

I learned another great lesson of faith from Sheila.

Sheila was a heroin addict, and tragically, she had contracted AIDS from a dirty needle.

Worse yet, she did not know she had AIDS for a few years. When she came to us for help, she came as a person with a heroin habit.

Because dirty needles transmit the AIDS virus, we offer to have our ladies tested. When Sheila went through the program, she was not experiencing any of the symptoms of AIDS. Therefore, she thought that she did not need to get tested.

We always leave that decision up to the ladies.

Sheila was such a wonderful gal. Elsie and I really loved her. She was a great inspiration and encouragement to the other ladies.

She reminded us a lot of Cindy, with the same kind of spirit that just reaches out to others.

And, like Cindy, Sheila went on to Bible school. She really enjoyed studying God's Word.

However, halfway through her first year,

she wasn't feeling well.

She went to the doctor. Because of her past drug habit, he immediately tested her for HIV.

The tragic news came back. Shelia had AIDS. And unfortunately, her condition was getting worse.

The doctor told Sheila the bad news. She had full-blown AIDS and was not expected to live more than thirty days.

There is medication that helps some AIDS patients, but it doesn't always work.

And it wasn't working for Sheila

When we heard the news, Elsie and I were shocked. It just seemed so unfair that this would happen to such a beautiful person, but sometimes the tragic events of life seem beyond understanding. We just have to trust God and His Wisdom.

Sheila decided to leave Bible school because she was so sick. She then came back to the Walter Hoving Home to say her final good-byes.

I knew she was coming. One of my human weaknesses is that I have a real hard time facing bad news. I would rather avoid it. It is extremely difficult for me to face such an intense personal tragedy as this.

But Sheila came, and although I knew she

was in our Home, I avoided her as best I could.

Not that I didn't love her, not that I didn't care, but it was just really tough for me to know that she was going to die within a couple of weeks, and this would be the last time that I would see her.

I needed time to prepare myself, not wanting to risk making her final days any more painful or difficult by some inadvertent weakness on my part.

Finally, I knew that I had to face her.

We were standing just inside the entranceway. Sheila said to me in a very soft, sincere voice, "I've come to tell you goodbye."

I knew what that meant. Soon, she was going to be dead, and I would never see her again on this earth.

I told Sheila that I was so sorry to hear what had happened to her. I was trying my best to encourage her, but again, as with Cindy, I just couldn't find the right words.

What do you say to a person who is dying?

I know, as a minister, I am supposed to talk about being absent from the body and being present with the Lord. I am supposed to say that we will spend eternity in heaven, and there will be no more sickness.

I had said that many times to other people who were sick, and had sincerely believed it.

But it just seemed so difficult for me to say that, as I faced this reality with Sheila.

As I looked at her withered body, once so vibrant and beautiful, I realized that in a couple of weeks she was going to be dead. I don't exactly recall what I was trying to say; just that I was speechless, stumbling for words which seemed adequate.

Bless her dear heart, Sheila came to my rescue.

She said, "Dad, you don't need to worry about me anymore. These last couple of years have been the best. I have lived them with Christ and soon I shall see him face to face. I'm looking forward to that moment."

Oh, God, such great faith!

I reached out and threw my arms around Sheila.

I don't know if you have ever hugged a person who is dying from AIDS, but it's the best hug that you could ever give. Really, you are just hugging bones. Sheila had become so skinny and frail. Someone described it as trying to hug a bicycle tire. All you feel are the spokes.

But with this hug, I could feel the loving pressure of Sheila's arms around my back, trying to reassure me that everything was okay.

Tragically, I was the one who was going to

live and face life with its unending problems, but Sheila would soon face Jesus, and be healed of her AIDS.

I don't know if you have ever heard of Joni Erickson. She is the girl who was crippled from a swimming accident, and started a worldwide ministry helping paraplegics. I'm a friend of this ministry, and when we're in California, Elsie and I and some of our ladies visit her quite often.

I was praying for Joni one day, praying that she would be healed. The Holy Spirit spoke to my heart, saying that when Joni passed from this life to the next, as she entered the Gates of Heaven, she would not be in a wheel chair but would walk straight through.

And, that is how Sheila felt about herself.

Finally, Sheila released her hug on me. I kissed her on the cheek. Then she walked outside and I headed towards my office.

I guess I just couldn't rise above that sacred moment with Sheila. As I walked into my office, I shut the door, walked over to the desk and sat down. I put my head on my desk and began to weep. I felt so sorry for Sheila and what she was facing. And, yet, I was so overwhelmed and feeling guilty because I did not have dying faith like Sheila.

I don't know how long I cried, but to this

day, I shall never forget those two momentous times in my life — Cindy in prison and Sheila dying of AIDS — both being greatly dignified through their faith.

Sitting here writing this book, I still weep. If I were to face prison or if I were to die with AIDS, would I have that kind of faith?

Oh, God, give me that faith. Give me that faith. Give me that faith.

CHAPTER 4

Trying to Stay Alive

This ministry can really get dangerous at times. The first time I almost got hurt took place up in the Bronx. It was late at night, and we were doing some witnessing on the streets. A number of ladies were out there on the streets, prostituting to support their drug habits.

I saw a girl on the corner and walked up to her, identifying myself. I told her about our ministry.

She said, "Oh, my God, man, I thought you were a trick." If you have not heard that before, a trick is a guy who the girl prostitutes with. I gave her a big smile and said, "No, Ma'am, I'm actually a minister."

Then she said, "Down the street, there, my old man is standing in a darkened doorway. He's signaling for me to bring you down there."

I was just about to say, "Well, that's great. Why don't we both walk down there and talk to him about the Lord. He needs to know Jesus, too!"

Before I could start speaking, she quickly blurted out, "He's got a big lead pipe in his hand, and as soon as you walk over, he's going to hit you over the head. Then, we're going to take your wallet, take your watch, even that wedding band on your hand."

My mouth flew open. I stared down the street. It was dark. I couldn't see anybody. But you better believe I was not about to doubt her story.

Now, let me tell you something. If it were my wife, Elsie, she would have said, "That's just great, but we'll be okay. The Lord will be with us."

And, Elsie would have grabbed that gal by her arm, and we would have marched down that street, ready to encounter that guy.

I hate to admit it, but I'm a "Chicken Christian." I do get scared on the streets, late at night in dangerous, high crime areas.

I suppose you think a man in my position should be full of faith, wisdom and power.

Ever hear about John the Baptist, and what happened to him?

How about Stephen, and all those stones?

Christians do get killed, and I just didn't feel like I was ready that night to get knocked unconscious or even killed by some guy with a big lead pipe.

So I quickly said, "I tell you, Ma'am, you do this. You go down there and tell him to come out here and let me have a few gentle words with him."

"Sure I will," she smiled, "I'll be right back."

I stood there watching her as she approached the darkened doorway... watching as she disappeared in the hellish shadows.

I squinted my eyes and saw nothing but darkness. I waited. Then I waited some more.

You guessed it. What kind of Christian am I really? If God were with Daniel in the lion's den, why wouldn't He be with me as I walked down that street?

I waited a while longer, but that precious little girl did not come back. These are really the ladies' pimps. When she did not bring me back down there, he might have used the lead pipe on her to punish her. Sadly, that kind of thing really happens.

I began to pray in the Spirit. I felt guilty. Then I confessed my unbelief.

After doing all that, you might think that I would have been prepared to walk down there boldly, grab that guy and tell him all about Jesus. But I did not.

I waited some more. I finally walked up the street where some of our staff was witnessing.

When I got home that night, I kept thinking about that girl. Suppose that guy killed her?

Or maybe he might have killed me? What would happen to this ministry? To Elsie? To our three children?

I honestly don't know whether I was right or wrong in how I handled the circumstances. I guess I just have to leave that to God.

About a month later, we received another lady in the program.

I knew I had seen her before. And then it hit me. It was the same girl I had contacted in the streets a few weeks ago.

I could not believe it!

I quickly walked up to her. She said, "Remember me?"

Remember? Are you kidding? I threw my arms around her and gave her a big hug. I thanked God that she was still alive.

I asked her what happened when she went down to her old man. She said, "Nothing." I took a deep breath. Thank God, I was spared.

The wonderful news is that Juanita went all the way through the program and graduated. She became a wonderful Christian and is now serving the Lord.

I have mentioned Elsie before, and now I must tell you my favorite story about her.

After we moved out to California and established that ministry, I was appointed as volunteer Chaplain at the California Institute of Women.

That is the California State Maximum Security State Prison in Chino, California. It is notorious because it is where the Manson killer gals are incarcerated.

My duty as a Chaplain was always on Saturday, and on this particular Saturday, it was Christmas Day. Elsie and I still went out to minister to the ladies on Christmas Evening.

One of my responsibilities as a Christian Chaplain was to escort church groups through all of the security systems. I had a huge ring of keys, and had to keep locking and unlocking doors to get these groups through.

A group was coming that night to minister to the ladies at the prison chapel, and I got the call they were at the gate. In order to get them, Elsie and I had to go through the whole process of all the locked doors.

We finally made it to the yard. As we were walking across the yard with the group, an officer yelled at me and said, "Come quick,

Chaplain! Could you please have a Christmas Service over here in this area?"

I looked over at the officer who stood in the doorway of what the ladies call "Killer Miller." It is the set of cells that house those who are in the penitentiary for murder. All of them are grouped together.

I yelled back to the officer, "I'm sorry, I don't have time for anybody else. I'm here with this church group, and we're slated for the chapel in a few moments."

The officer was desperate. "Please, Chaplain! Please, Chaplain! Don't you have anybody to come over here? This is Christmas! And, it would be so wonderful if these prisoners had a chapel service!"

"Killer Miller" was a lockdown place most of the time, and those inmates could not come to our chapel service. I knew that.

Elsie was next to me, and I yelled back to the officer, "The only other person I've got here with me is my wife." The officer yelled back, "We'll take her! We'll take her!"

I looked at Elsie. She had a big smile on her face. Did she really know what it would be like to go to "Killer Miller" and see all of those convicted murderers? I am sure that did not enter her mind.

I told the officer I would go ahead and get

the chapel service set up with the volunteer church group, and then I would come on over.

After I made those arrangements, Elsie and I headed toward "Killer Miller." Again with the keys, I unlocked one door, stepped through it and locked that one. Then I went through another one, unlocked it, and then another one.

The only place available for the chapel service was in the laundry room. I had to go through some more locked doors. They really locked these women up!

Finally, we got to the laundry room and unlocked that door.

In a few moments the ladies came. There were no chairs, no pulpits, no pews, no nothing, just some washing machines and a concrete floor.

Elsie, bless her heart, was in the height of her glory. She had the ladies come in and sit on the floor. I told Elsie I would be back after our service.

Now, here's the tough part. I had to lock the door behind Elsie. She was locked in with all of these murderers.

I went through the lock systems again and on over to the chapel. We had a wonderful service with many of the ladies.

Christmas is such a sad time for these

ladies, and there are a lot of tears. They were missing their families, and a lot of them were missing their children.

After the service, I went back to get Elsie. I had no idea what to expect.

My tension built as I slipped one by one through all the locked doors. Finally, from the laundry room, I opened the door.

Sure enough, there was Elsie, sitting in the middle of the floor, with a huge smile on her face, surrounded by all of those ladies.

Elsie is fearless.

In almost fifty years of marriage, Elsie and I have lived in a number of different homes. The most wonderful place that we ever lived was in the ghetto in Brooklyn, a high crime area.

In spite of those circumstances, Elsie still thought she had died and gone to heaven. She loves danger. I guess it is just her faith in God!

It is truly amazing! What great encouragement it is to me, and certainly to many others.

After we moved from Brooklyn up to Garrison, we still faced life and death situations.

Other than almost getting killed by Joe Loco, I guess the second biggest threat I faced was when these four guys came to kill me.

This is what happened.

There was a lady in our program named Corrine. She seemed to do be doing well, until one day; while out on a pass she went and got drunk. We had to deal with her behavior when she came back. Sometimes we dismiss them if their attitude is not right, but when we confronted her, she took it well.

On her next pass, however, she got drunk again.

This time we had no choice but to dismiss her. To tolerate her continued rebellious behavior would have put the other ladies in jeopardy.

After she left the Home, she called me and said she had called her son, and that he was coming over with three other guys to kill me.

Of course, I had been threatened before in my life. Possibly, you have too.

Sometimes it is bogus. Sometimes it is not.

It all depends upon who is trying to kill you.

I didn't know if I should believe what she was saying. But then she said, "If you let me back in, I'll tell them not to come."

Of course, I told her I would not let her come back, not under any kind of threat like that. She hung up the phone on me.

About a week later, Corrine called again.

She said, "My son and four guys are coming Saturday morning, and they are going to kill you. They have guns, and they are going to get you good."

By this time, Corrine was sober and she really seemed determined that she was going to get back at me for not letting her back in. Still, I couldn't bow to that kind of pressure, otherwise I'd have the lunatics running the asylum, as they say.

I tried to explain to Corrine that this was not the way to settle differences.

She would hear none of it.

Hanging up the phone, I wondered what I should do. Should I call the police?

Suppose it was just a bluff on Corrine's part? I didn't want to look stupid. And yet, I didn't want to be stupid.

I kept praying about it. It just seemed I couldn't get any answer.

Saturday morning came. On Saturday mornings, the ladies usually get up and cook a special breakfast at about 9:30.

It's their day off, and some of them love to cook. We usually have pancakes, sausage, eggs and bacon.

I let the ladies know about the threats from Corrine.

Some got really shook up, but others kind of laughed about it. I think they were pretty well evenly divided about what would happen.

But still, some of the ladies kept a lookout toward the driveway to see if anybody would be coming up that road. I really didn't eat much breakfast, as I was nervous.

What would I do if they came? I certainly didn't want to endanger these ladies if there was going to be a shooting.

Maybe I should just run off, and come back tomorrow. Then I thought that if those guys came, and I was not here, and they were armed, they might shoot one of the ladies or (God forbid) even Elsie! I decided to stick around.

Suddenly one of the ladies shouted, "Here they come!"

I immediately jumped up. I was in the front room, looking up the driveway and here came four guys.

I knew who it was. They had arrived.

My heart was beating like crazy, and I was having trouble catching my breath. To this day, I don't know why I did what I did.

Without thinking, I darted out the front door and went across the parking lot. As I approached them they jumped out of the car.

I shall never forget this one guy. He kind of had a "John Wayne" hands-on-hip stance. I probably knew that he was the one packing a gun.

Before anyone said anything, I went up to the leader and stuck out my hand and said, "Hey, guys! We were waiting for you, we've got pancakes, eggs, bacon, sausage, you name it, good coffee, too! Come on in and have breakfast with us!"

I let go of the guy's hand, and started pulling him toward the front door. As I turned around and looked at the front door, there were a whole bunch of ladies standing there.

I think that if something had happened, they were ready to come to Dad's rescue. I shall never forget that support from them.

Much to my amazement, those four guys started walking toward the front door. It was almost as though a trance came over them. Still, no one had said a word to me.

I knew what was happening. The power of the Holy Spirit was on those men, and they couldn't resist it.

If you have ever been to the Walter Hoving Home, you will notice something different about us. If you are a Christian, you can sense the presence of Christ when you come into our Home whether it's in Garrison, New York or Pasadena, California.

His presence has always been there, and I shall be eternally grateful that Jesus lives with us.

As soon as we all got to the steps, the ladies started telling those guys how glad they were to see them and how great it was for them to come.

Some of the ladies grabbed the guys by the arms and took them into the dining room, sat them down and told them they would be serving them.

It almost seemed like a dream. Everything was magically falling into place. No one had pulled a gun, at least not yet.

I sat down next to the leader of the group and explained to him what had happened to his mother and why we had to ask her to leave. I apologized about what had taken place and I told him that we continued to pray for his mother, Corrine.

He told me, "My mother is very special to me. I'd do anything she asked me to do."

I knew what she had asked him to do, go and kill John Benton, the President of the Walter Hoving Home.

Then I just began to tell them about Jesus. The Spirit of God was continuing to work, and I could see that he and his friends were moved.

Thank God, there is a happy ending to this story. I'm still here!

Corrine's son and his three friends left,

well fed and challenged by the gospel. And, to this day, I've never heard from them again.

While we were in California, I drove down to MacArthur Park late one night to see if any ladies were on the streets.

In California, we do a lot of witnessing in the most dangerous areas, and always feel lucky to get out alive. Gang members and pimps are known to commit murder.

As I drove through one heavy gang area, which is especially violent, I kept looking to see if I could find a lady.

Suddenly my car chugged and lurched. Then the engine stopped.

I knew that the car was on its last legs, but our finances were tough, so I still hung onto it. I had driven it over 150,000 miles.

I tried to get it going again, but no luck. The engine would not turn.

Looking around, there were suspicious looking people everywhere. I knew that in this drug-infested area there were all kinds of problems.

Gang members were prevalent. This was the area of the notorious Fourth Street Gang. They would kill anybody. They robbed and controlled prostitution.

Everybody was terrified of them, including me!

I sat there, pondering my situation, wondering how the Lord was going to save me this time.

I'm no mechanic, but I figured that maybe there was a loose wire, or something. I quickly got out of the car, opened the hood and checked the wires. They seemed to be okay.

I noticed a homeless man pushing a cart, coming toward me. He said, "Hey, buddy, got a problem?"

I said, "Yeah, my car stalled and won't start."

He said, "I'm a mechanic. Let me take a look at it."

Of course, every homeless person in the world is a mechanic. I thought if this guy got under the hood of my car, Lord only knows what kind of a mess he might make. But what choice did I have?

He looked around, and then pulled a piece of wire out of his cart. He stuck it down in the engine well and said, "Try it now!"

I couldn't figure out what the guy was doing, but as I got behind the wheel of the car and turned the key. Would you believe it? The engine roared to life!

I jumped out of the car, reached into my wallet, grabbed a twenty-dollar bill, slammed it into the guy's hand and said; "You don't know how much I appreciate this!"

He stood there with a big smile.

I took off and soon arrived home safely. Explain this one to me! So help me, God, I don't know what that guy did.

Maybe he was an angel? I don't know if angels take courses in auto mechanics, but whoever the Lord used, it was good enough for me. I'm still alive, today!

I do believe that God will protect us until our time has come. I will try to do my best to bring the gospel to these ladies, even though at times it may cost me my life.

I always claim this scripture in moments of great fear: "Absent from the body is to be present with the Lord." I do hope, though, it won't happen tomorrow. I feel that I still have a few more years left, and so many ladies to minister to.

CHAPTER 5

Sometimes Things Can Get Weird Around Here

I shall never forget Jean. Very attractive, very petite, a little under five feet. The only thing big about her was her smile — a big gorgeous smile. Unfortunately, Jean was on heroin and her addiction was destroying her natural beauty.

When she came to us, she had a long run of using heroin. Kicking cold turkey was a real challenge to her. It is always torture to watch someone go through withdrawal, lots of vomiting, hot and cold flashes, diarrhea and unendurable pain.

Elsie was very helpful, though. During these times of severe pain and agony, Elsie would rub Jean's back. Jean really seemed to appreciate it, and was able to kick cold turkey. She then started her newfound journey in the Christian life.

About three weeks into the program, Jean was in Chapel. All of a sudden, she jumped up and ran outside, down to the street. We started after her, but I couldn't catch her. Like that, she was gone.

How tragic, here this young lady, with seemingly tremendous potential, was gone from us. It is always hard to take when the ladies leave.

A young man, Al Samuelson, was with us that morning. He was a former addict. Today he is an outstanding Bible teacher and evangelist. After service, Al came and explained to me what happened to Jean. He said, "Jean is not a girl."

I nearly passed out! I could not believe that this cute little gal who Elsie gave some of our daughter's clothes to, was actually a man.

"You know that, Al?" I asked.

Al kind of giggled, "I spent time with him in jail. I know all about him."

The other staff ladies found out what had happened, some were shocked, some laughed. Of course, I went back to Elsie. When I told her what had happened, she couldn't believe it either.

Then I remembered. She had been rubbing this guy's back in the middle of the night.

"Could you tell he was a guy?" I asked.

"Honey, there is absolutely no way I knew she was a guy. Of course, he didn't show me the front part of his body, but backs are backs, whether it is a girl or a boy."

Elsie and I laughed together. I guess this ministry does have weird people. But the story didn't end there.

About two o'clock that morning, the telephone rang. Answering it, I identified myself. The voice on the end of the line said, "This is Jean."

I gasped! How dare that guy call me, especially after pulling off that stunt with us?

"I wonder if I could come and talk to you?" he asked.

Should I tell him I knew about him or should I just wait and see? I decided to wait.

"Why don't you come and meet me in my office tomorrow morning at ten?" I said.

"I'm desperate! If I don't find help, I'm going to kill myself! Please! Please! Please help me!"

Despite his charade, the desperation in his voice was real. It was heart breaking.

"Could I come right now?" he asked again.

As I mentioned, this ministry is a ministry that operates seven days a week, twenty-four hours a day, 365 days a year. We are always here to help.

So I said, "Okay, you can come now."

He said, "I'll be there in about half an hour."

I got dressed and went down to the front room. About a half-hour went by and sure enough, there was Jean at the doorway.

I invited him in. I thought I had better not play cat and mouse with this guy, and just blurted out what I knew.

"Jean, I know you're not a girl. You're a boy pretending to be one."

He put his head down. There was a long pause. I saw tears running down his cheeks.

He said, "It's not all that easy. You see, I really am a girl. A girl with male sex organs."

"Yeah, sure," I said, "God made male and female, and I don't think God gets mixed up."

I was at least relieved when Jean confessed to me that he really was a girl with the parts of a man. Had there been a big argument, the only way I would have known for sure would be for him to expose himself. I certainly didn't want that!

Jean began to cry some more. He said, "Dad B, I want to tell you what has happened to my life. When I was a young child, I didn't want to play with fire engines or with the boys. I wanted to play with dolls. I didn't want to play football or any of those other kinds of boys' sports. I just wanted to do what the girls did. I knew deep inside of me that something was wrong. I tried to be a boy, but it didn't work. So I decided to be a girl."

Jean sounded convincing. Was I being swayed by his tears, or was this really what he was?

He said, "I just couldn't figure myself out. I tried everything. I tried to be a boy. I really tried! That didn't satisfy me. I tried being a girl, but trying to live that lifestyle is like living in hell, and then, I tried to kill myself, a number of times, but, I didn't even succeed at that."

When Jean started talking about suicide, I knew I had a desperate person on my hands. "Do you believe me?" he asked.

That kind of caught me off guard. That was my first experience with what is now commonly known as a transvestite, a guy who impersonates a woman.

I said, "I believe that what you have told me, as far as your feelings are concerned, is what has happened to you. I can understand that you have lived a very frustrating life."

He said, "I've finally made the decision to have a sex organ change. My doctor is Doctor Bernstein at Columbia University and he is preparing me for a sex change."

I knew I had him. He was making this up. "Can I talk to your doctor?" I asked.

Jean said, "He does this quite often. He is

very famous. I know he'll talk to you."

"How can I get hold of him?"

"I'll give you his number. You can call him and confirm what I am trying to tell you. Honest, Dad B, I'm really a girl." Jean gave me the telephone number.

He asked, "Can you still help me?"

I was really stuck. Could I bring Jean into the Home as a guy? That wouldn't work, it was against our charter rules.

Should I send him to the Teen Challenge Boys' Home? I could just imagine how those boys would feel having this guy in the room who says he is really a girl. That wouldn't work either.

"I'll do my best and see what I can do to help you, Jean. I will see this Doctor Bernstein, and then I'll let you know if we can help," I told him.

That seemed to satisfy Jean and he got up to leave. At least it settled the problem of him asking me to stay here with the girls. I told him to call me in three or four days and I would talk to him then.

Before he left, I prayed with Jean, and this was a tough prayer. What do you pray?

I prayed saying that no matter whether boy or girl, Jesus loves everyone and I knew that Jesus had a very special love for Jean. He broke down and cried some more.

He said, "Good bye," and I headed back to bed. It all seemed like some kind of weird nightmare.

I'd never seen this type of person before, and this one had been so convincing. I did not know it then, but later I would run into a few more people like this in the ministry.

The following day, I called Columbia University and spoke to Doctor Bernstein. Surprisingly, he was very friendly and said that he definitely knew Jean and yes, Jean was a patient of his.

I asked if I could meet with him, and he quickly agreed.

A couple of days later I was in his office at Columbia University. Doctor Bernstein very patiently explained to me the problem that some people like Jean have. It is almost a freak of nature.

These people are true transsexuals, not simply role-playing transvestites. He said that actually the hormones are female, making them women with male sex organs. He was very convincing.

I was very confused. Is this what really happens? God makes people such as this? Honestly, I did not know what to believe. I went back home and waited for Jean's call.

Sure enough, he called me.

I explained that I had met with Doctor Bernstein, and I didn't know what to do. I said I needed more time for prayer. I asked Jean to call me back in a couple of days. He said that he would.

The next day, as we were discussing Jean once again with some of our ladies, one of the ladies began to laugh.

I asked, "Do you know Jean?"

"Sure, I did Dad B. In fact, Jean and I used to live together. That guy's no woman. He's all man. You know what I mean?"

I knew what she meant. Jean had sexual relations with this gal. That convinced me. Jean was a man. He never did call back though. To this day, I do not know where he is. One thing I do know is that no matter what he is up to, Jesus still loves him and Jesus really wants to save him.

That wasn't the last time I encountered something weird.

After moving up to Garrison, one day I received a telephone call from a pastor. He told me about his church in New York City and claimed it was "one of the largest churches in America."

The Pastor said, "Mr. Benton, I was wondering if my daughter and I could come up and talk to you? My daughter tried to kill herself again, and we desperately need help. Could we please come see you?"

I have great sympathy for pastors. Not only because I once was a pastor, but also because pastoring churches today is one of the most difficult challenges anyone could face.

Through the years, we have helped pastors' daughters. I have cried with many of these fathers over their wayward daughters. At another time a pastor of one of the largest churches in Texas had called me. He said that he was a success at everything. His church was huge; he had won many people to Christ, but he was a complete failure as a father to his daughter. He sent his daughter to us, and thank God, today she is an outstanding Christian. And, her father is so proud of her now.

Now, here was a pastor from New York City coming to me with his daughter. Over the phone, we made arrangements for this pastor to come in with his daughter. When he walked into my office, I wasn't quite prepared for what walked in. Instead of bringing me his daughter, he brought me his son.

Sometimes I forget things, and I thought about what he had said in the previous telephone conversation. We certainly were talking about his daughter, not his son. Maybe the daughter wouldn't come, and they were bringing the son to help out. I was so confused.

After introducing ourselves, the Pastor turned towards me and said, "Reverend Benton, this is my daughter Pam."

I took a look at Pam. Pam had no remote resemblance to a girl. She was wearing overalls, men's work shoes, a goatee and a hair cut just like a guy.

We sat down and the pastor began to tell me the story. When Pam was a small girl, she had no desire to play with dolls. She was the exact opposite of Jean.

Pam wanted to play with boys' toys. Very athletic, she grew up playing sports with the boys, and was very good at it too!

The Pastor said, "Looking back now, I think I made a mistake. When Pam was eighteen years old, she once again told me that she felt she was a boy, not a girl."

"I said, 'Honey, do whatever you want to do.' That's when Pam went out and decided to become a man. She got a job in a construction company. She began to take male hormones, which caused her to grow a beard. Then she started wearing a chest suppressor, and for the last three years this is what she's looked like."

Pam sat there with a very serious face. Up to this point, she had said nothing. She seemed to be quite nice, and evidently she wanted help or she would not have been here.

The pastor continued, "After that, serious problems began to develop. Pam became highly suicidal and tried to kill herself. That didn't work, so she turned to drugs. Now, she is hooked on drugs. Reverend Benton, can you please help Pam?"

I had failed with Jean. Was this going to be another failure?

I knew one thing. I was going to do my very best for this dear pastor.

There was a long pause. The pastor began to cry. That really got to me. I started to cry along with him. I looked at Pam. She too was weeping.

Life can be so complicated, with such grief. And, this pastor was experiencing it . . . with his very own daughter.

"Pam, do you want help?" I asked.

She nodded. "Please help me! Please help me!"

Well, we took Pam into the program. We told her she would have to dress like a girl and really change her lifestyle.

A funny thing happened that evening. One of the ladies came running out in her bathrobe, screaming at the top of her voice.

She ran up to me and said, "Dad, Dad, come quick! There is a guy in our bathroom, and he's shaving. I actually saw him. Come quick!"

I laughed and said, "Honey, that's actually a girl who is going to change her lifestyle."

"You're kidding? That's really a girl?" I reassured this young lady, again.

Pam settled into our program. She quit taking the male hormones, and her breasts began to grow. She stopped growing whiskers, and she really wanted to serve God.

During wintertime in Garrison, we get lots of snow. One afternoon as I was walking from the main building over to the new house, Pam came bursting out the front door screaming at the top of her lungs. I mean, a blood curdling scream.

I tried to stop her, but she was kind of big.

I yelled for her to stop, but she kept on running. She ran down past the main house. Snow was everywhere. She ran on down towards the main entrance, with me chasing her, again, yelling for her to stop.

But she wouldn't listen to me.

All of a sudden she turned and headed towards the woods. I went after her. I fell into some branches and skinned myself. My head was buried in the snow.

When I looked up, I couldn't see Pam. I thought to myself that enough was enough. If she really wanted help, she would come back.

Later on, she did come back.

I asked Pam what had happened. She said, "I was taught in therapy that when things begin to build up, to let out a scream. It's called primal therapy. You just start screaming."

I told Pam that at our house, when frustration builds up, we don't start screaming. We start praying. I taught her the value of personal, closet prayer to relieve the burdens out there in the world.

Thank God, from that day forward, there were no more screaming incidents with Pam. I know that she found great help in personal prayer. Pam graduated from the program. She assumed the characteristics of a fine young woman of God, moved to the Midwest and began serving the Lord.

After graduation, Pam came back East and called Elsie and me. She wanted to take us out to dinner. We met in New York City, and as I sat across the table, I could not believe my eyes. What a beautiful woman. God did work a miracle in her life. And, today her dad is so proud of her. Thank God, the Lord does work!

I know a lot has been said and written about the problem of homosexuality. Out on the streets I've run into more transvestites — guys who look like girls.

In fact, of all the types of people on the street, the transvestites seem more responsive to the gospel of love, almost more than anybody else does. I still witness to them about Jesus.

I do believe the sin of homosexuality is plainly taught in God's Word. So are the other sins of adultery, stealing, lying, cheating and so forth.

Sometimes I think, however, that we hate the homosexual more than his sin. We've got to be careful of that.

But, no matter what a person is trying to become, or has become, Jesus still loves them and can change their lives.

I have seen it happen!

CHAPTER 6

I'M GOING TO STUFF GEORGE MUELLER FULL OF RICE

Ever hear of George Mueller? As I understand it, many years ago in England, he opened up an orphanage that later housed hundreds of children.

George Mueller was a Godly man, and he trusted God to supply all of his needs.

As the story goes, when George got down to just one slice of bread he would gather everybody to pray and miraculously, there would be a knock on the door and a huge basketful of food would appear, enough to feed all of those orphans.

George Mueller wrote a book about all the miracles that happened to him, and when you read about him your faith knows no bounds.

I read the book.

Now here is what upsets me about dear old George.

In 1956, Elsie and I went to Japan as missionaries. At that time we were members of an independent church by the name of Bethel

Temple, in downtown Seattle.

Elsie and I were raised in this church. In fact, we were in the nursery together. I do not think it was love at first sight, but it was pretty soon after that when we fell in love with each other. We have been married since 1952.

We felt the call of God to go to Japan. Since we were promised very little support from Bethel Temple, we sold everything we had in order to raise enough money to get there.

As we made our plans for the trip, I expected the best. The reports we had from other missionaries indicated that Japan was dying and going to hell. They were just waiting for someone like me to come and save them.

Our mission's station was situated between Tokyo and Yokohama.

It was a strategic location because that was the base from which I was going to win both of those cities for the Lord.

The date came and we arrived in Japan.

From day one, all that we hoped and dreamed for in Japan began to fall apart.

We arrived in Japan during the worst possible month. It was terribly hot and humid. Getting off the plane, we felt as though we were walking into an oven. That was tough.

Things got worse.

We were given a very small one-room house. Elsie and I arrived there with our daughter. Elsie was pregnant as well. We made provisions with the hospital to care for the birth of our next child.

Since the hospital was about two and one half hours away, the doctor monitoring Elsie's condition decided to take her by induction.

God blessed us with a beautiful son. He had red hair, and we named him after a dear friend of mine, Jerry.

However, there was a problem. When Jerry was born, only one of his lungs worked properly. He was placed under emergency care in order to try and get the other lung to inflate.

I went home that night on the train, deeply troubled by this terrible turn of events.

When I got back to the hospital the next day, I noticed that the doctor and some of the nurses were running out of the room where Jerry 's incubator was.

I asked the nurse how things were coming. She said that they were doing the best they could. I could tell by the tone of her voice that it was not good.

I went to see Elsie. She told me that they brought Jerry to her, but after he cried, he started gasping for air. They took him out of her arms and placed him in the other room.

I went out to another room to wait, and I really began to pray. I could not believe that God would do this to me. Elsie and I had sold everything to come to Japan, and now this.

I knew somehow that Jerry just had to live.

After praying and seeking God, the doctor came through the door. I looked at his face. He was not smiling.

He walked over to me, put his hand on my shoulder and said, "I'm sorry, Reverend Benton."

"What happened?" I asked.

"Your son has just died," he told me. I wanted to scream out at God, but I held it inside.

I went in to see Elsie. I told her what had happened. We threw our arms around each other and began to weep. I could not understand how a good God could do this to us.

Things got even worse.

In Japan, they believe in cremation by law, but foreigners are permitted a typical American burial.

The next day a missionary friend of mine came and picked up Jerry's little body in a tiny casket. We put the casket in the trunk of his car and drove to the Yokohama International

Cemetery.

The burial was so crude. I had to carry the shovel that dug the soil to bury his body.

After a brief ceremony, we placed the casket in the ground and the cemetery workers threw dirt on top of his casket.

As I stood there, looking down at my son being buried like this, I began to cry again.

Elsie was still in the hospital. After another week, she came home.

In my heart, I began to make preparations to return to America. I wasn't about to backslide and get away from God, but this missionary bit was all that I could take.

No more of this stuff for me.

I returned to our little mission station, and was in my office on my knees, still weeping.

I've never done this before and haven't done it since, but as I began to open my Bible the Holy Spirit guided me to the words of the Apostle Paul when he said, . . . that I might finish my ministry with joy."

I asked the Lord if that could be my testimony also, and I felt the presence of the Lord and peace came into my troubled heart. Elsie and I decided to stay in Japan.

We were there two years when Elsie's dad passed away.

Her mother started to die, too. The

Mission Board called Elsie home to attend the funeral of her father, and to be with her mother. When her mother did not improve the Mission Board decided that I should come home as well.

Once home, I was with one of my brothers, Doug, who asked me the obvious question, "How did things go in Japan?"

Of course, Doug knew about the death of our son, but what he did not know was my philosophy about George Mueller.

One of the things that George Mueller did was that he never told anybody about his need. He only told God. Evidently, George had a ton of faith, and God came through every time for him.

What my brother Doug didn't know, was that we had almost starved to death. We were not bringing enough money in to support ourselves.

In fact, it had gotten so bad one day that we did not have enough money for any food at all, nothing.

I had to humble myself and ask one of the elders of the church, this dear Japanese man, if he could give me enough rice for supper.

That was one of the most humiliating experiences I have ever had, but it was what I had to do to stay alive.

I told Doug what happened, how we had almost starved to death. He looked at me and said, "John, you are a big fool. Had you written to me, I certainly would have sent you money."

While in Japan, I never ever wrote to anybody asking for money. Again, standing on the principle of George Mueller, God knew our needs and He would have to supply it.

It worked for George Mueller, but it did not work for me.

I learned a great lesson. We as Christians must be very careful and not try to pattern our lives after how God deals with other people.

Please do not misunderstand me. I really believe that's what God led George Mueller to do, and that was simply: write no letters; talk to no one; just call on God.

And that is how God personally worked with George Mueller.

After reflecting upon what had happened to us in Japan, I have had a different approach to raising funds for this ministry.

The Book of James tells us that James said, "You have not because you ask not." In fact, Jesus said, "Ask and it shall be given unto you."

I do not believe in begging for money, but I do believe that many people want to know what our needs are all about, and that they will really respond if they have an opportunity to see the needs of The Walter Hoving Home.

And that is not to say that God does not still work miraculously.

David Wilkerson taught me another lesson.

He said, "If God closes a door, it only means one thing. He has a bigger one to open up."

In my book, "*One Lady At A Time*," I explained in more detail how we got this beautiful Garrison estate where we live today and where we minister to many, many ladies.

It is an interesting story since we thought we were getting the estate across the street from where we are now.

I knew for sure that God was going to give us that first estate, until He mysteriously shut that door. Not knowing at the time, that God had a beautiful, huge estate across the street for us.

That is where we live today.

When Elsie, our three children and me were living in the main house in the Garrison mansion, we were having trouble trying to function as a family.

Elsie and I were having some personal problems, I went to Dave Wilkerson, again, and told him about some of the challenges we were facing.

Dave told me that Elsie, our three children, and me had to move out of the house. That we needed to build a separate home for our family, right there on the campus.

I told Dave that I didn't think that was a good idea, because we were trying to save up enough money to build another home for more ladies.

Dave told me, "John, if you provide for your family, God will provide all of the rest of the money for a home."

We decided to go ahead and build a three bedroom home for ourselves, and God did miraculously supply that. Would you believe, after that home was completed, we got a very large grant from a dear friend and we built the additional home for the ladies?

God does work miracles. And God continues to provide for Elsie and me.

Our three children are all grown and married now. They are all serving the Lord, as well as their children. Elsie and I have maintained a simple lifestyle.

In Garrison, New York, we live in a small two-bedroom home on the campus.

In Pasadena, California, we live in another small two bedroom house in the back of the hotel.

This is our choice, to live rather simply, as it gives us more opportunity to devote more of our attention and time to the ministry and to the ladies.

We have been honored in many different ways, and sometimes undeservedly so. It is really the staff that God has given to us who carry the heavy burden ministering to the needs of these ladies.

I will have to tell you about a little incident with which I have been honored.

In California, on my day off, I get a little vain.

I go down to the Ritz Carlton Hotel and have breakfast. I purchase a *New York Times* newspaper and sit by the pool, eating my breakfast. It is a time to get away, and I really enjoy those moments.

When you drive up to the entrance of the hotel, the attendants immediately take your car and park it.

I got acquainted with one of the young men there, and the next time I came, he took my car and said, "Good morning, Dr. Benton. It is good to have you back again."

When this attendant said, "Dr. Benton," he said it rather loudly. I noticed that people turned and looked toward me.

I smiled, I wanted to say, "I'm not really a

Doctor, I'm just a plain ordinary preacher, who is trying to do something for God." But at times I am rather shy, so I didn't say anything.

After breakfast, when I came out to get my car, the same young man said, "Dr. Benton, just one moment please. We'll have your car." Again, people looked at me.

I noticed that this young man had parked my car, not in the regular parking area, but up near the entrance in a special place.

And so, every time I would go to the Ritz Carlton, I was always Dr. Benton, and had a special place to park my car.

I kind of felt guilty to be called Dr. Benton. I told Elsie how they called me Dr. Benton and that I had better tell them not to.

Elsie had a better answer.

She said, "Honey, they give honorary degrees to Billy Graham and they call him Dr. Billy Graham; they give honorary degrees to Bill Bright and they call him Dr. Bill Bright. Why don't you just think of it as the Ritz Carlton Hotel giving you an honorary degree and that's why they call you Dr. Benton?" I thought about that. And, of course, Elsie has great wisdom and insight, so I accepted her answer.

Occasionally though, I think it is kind of vain of me. Don't you?

CHAPTER 7

MINISTERS DO TWICE AS MUCH

Bill Brown is a personal friend of mine. At the time I met him, he was the Chairman of the New York City Billy Graham Crusade. My goodness, this was way back in about 1967, if I remember correctly.

Bill later became President of World Wide Pictures, which is the film company of the Billy Graham Evangelistic Association.

I met Bill after the crusade and heard they wanted to sell the office furniture from the crusade office in New York City. We had just moved to Garrison and were in desperate need of office supplies.

When I went with Bill into New York City, he showed me around the office and told me that everything had to go. Remember the old manual typewriters?

There were a bunch of those, plus desks, chairs, pencils, pencil sharpeners, stationery, ink, pens, everything we needed!

Billy Graham was a personal friend of

Walter Hoving. Walter had supported Billy throughout the years. I told Bill what we were doing; he seemed interested. I asked him how much it would cost to buy everything in the office.

Bill had a big smile on his face and said, "$1,900."

Bill has always had a big heart, and he certainly was looking out for us. We took everything there.

What a blessing it was to be able to use all of that office equipment in Garrison. We cleared the second story of the garage, did some remodeling and that became our office. What a great blessing!

But, that wasn't the end of Bill Brown.

His wife, Joan, is an author. Occasionally Elsie and I would meet Bill and Joan at the Christian Booksellers Convention or other book related events.

By this time, Bill had been appointed the President of World Wide Pictures and lived in California. He kept saying, "John, why don't you come out to California and start another Walter Hoving Home. There's plenty of girls and plenty of money."

Well I certainly was interested in plenty of girls and plenty of money, but at that time, we were still trying to develop the ministry of the

Walter Hoving Home - Pasadena, CA

The Staff and Girls in Pasadena

Walter Hoving Home - Garrison, NY

The Staff and Girls in Garrison

Walter Hoving Home in Garrison, New York.

I gave Bill the spiritual answer that a lot of people give me, "I'll pray about it."

Honestly, I really didn't pray that much about it, because all of my energy at that time was involved in helping more ladies and developing the program in Garrison.

But Bill would not give up. Every time I saw him, he kept saying the same thing. "Come to California."

One day I was sitting at my desk, thanking the Lord for all He had done for the Walter Hoving Home in Garrison. Our home now was filled with girls and we were rejoicing in much success. These ladies who had been so terribly bound in drugs and alcohol were now set free.

I put my feet up on the desk, looked around the office and said, "This is really the way to live."

Then my dream was shattered. The still small voice said, "What about California?"

I have never actually heard the audible voice of God, but I have heard the distinct voice of the Spirit speaking to me many times. I am not a mystical type, you might have heard a few of these people who seem like God is talking to them all day long.

I've met a few of these strange people and

I've often wondered if God had tried to tell them what they were supposed to do. Maybe God was mixed up or something.

There is a definite voice of the Spirit and a voice of the mind. But believe me, sometimes it is difficult to distinguish between the two.

After that encounter with God in my office, my spirit was getting restless. I'm the type of person who has to be busy all of the time. I keep looking for opportunities to do more for God.

By this time, the Home had developed into a well-managed ministry and the staff carried many responsibilities, and handled them very efficiently. I found myself with open spaces during the day. Nothing to do. And let me tell you, that bugs the life out of me!

Again the still small voice spoke.

This time it was louder, "What about California?"

After much prayer, I finally yielded to that voice and called Bill Brown.

He was excited. Bill said that he would set up some luncheons for us to discuss the launching of the program.

Elsie and I made arrangements to fly to California. Bill had these luncheons waiting for us. There was interest, and we kept praying about whether or not this is what we should do.

Some people ask me why we made Pasadena the location of the Walter Hoving Home in California.

I wish I could tell them that God spoke audibly and said, "Pasadena." Or that there was a lightning bolt from heaven, and it burned a hole in the map that I was looking at.

Unfortunately, none of these things happened. I just looked at a map of Greater Los Angeles, and thought that Pasadena would be nice. I knew about the Rose Parade and the Rose Bowl and little else.

So, I said to myself, "This is it."

On one of the trips to California, I decided to spend some of my time on the streets. You have probably heard all about Sunset Boulevard, as had I. It's certainly been featured in the media enough with all of the prostitutes out on Sunset Boulevard.

I drove the length of Sunset Boulevard. Back and forth. No ladies.

I felt so discouraged. Where in the world were they? Was Bill really right? Were there really a lot of ladies here in California who needed help?

We had another luncheon, then went back to Garrison, New York.

Later, we came back out to California.

Again, I drove along Sunset Boulevard. And there, can you believe it, was a lady sitting at a bus stop. I could tell by the way that she looked at the cars driving by that she was out prostituting.

I turned the corner, parked my car, jumped out, ran toward the lady, and said, "Hello I am John Benton of the Walter Hoving Home. We're here to help ladies like you."

She glared at me. And then she said, "I don't blankety blank care who you are, or where the blankety blank you are from. Get the blankety blank out of here." I will let you fill in the blankety blanks. I could not believe how she was cussing me out.

"You don't understand," I refused to give up, "My wife and I have a Home in Garrison, New York, which is called the Walter Hoving Home. We're here to start another one. We want to help you."

She screamed at me, "Didn't you get the message, Mister? I said, get the blankety blank out of here!"

She took a step or two towards me, and then cussed at me some more. People were looking. I didn't want to cause a disturbance, so I just politely said, "I'm sorry."

I walked away got into my car and slowly drove off. One thing for sure, ladies in California were certainly mean and ornery. Although I wasn't sure how many there were, they definitely were a handful.

We decided to launch the program. The first thing we did was rent a small three bedroom place and rustle up three staff members. We would start out by evangelizing. Visiting the streets and going to the jails were our top priorities.

After moving to California, we soon found out that there were many, many ladies. Through a contact with the Los Angeles Police Department, I was able to go out undercover with the vice squad.

The sergeant showed me where all the ladies were. They were there, in the jails. Literally, thousands and thousands of ladies were in jails in California. To this very day, Elsie and I go every month to the jails, and sometimes to the streets.

With the launching of any new program, you always encounter many challenges. If you have read my book "*One Lady At A Time*," you know the enormous problems we faced when we began the ministry in New York. California was no different.

When we rented the house, it was small. In fact, when Elsie and I first came out to California from Garrison, we had no bedroom of our own. We took a mattress and laid it on the living room floor and that was our bedroom. We shared a bathroom with the other staff.

I'm kind of a private person, and this was a tough ordeal, but we had to start somewhere. So, we slept on the floor on a mattress. Then we found a house to rent where we could care for eight ladies at a time.

It was in a nice area, and fortunately, Elsie and I were able to have our own bedroom. However, we still had to share our bathroom with another staff member. The walls were thin in this house, so this was a real challenge.

So help me, when the other staff member went into the bathroom I never knew what took her so long.

Growing up, and some of you might remember this; we had a Sears catalog that we used in the outhouse. You could sit there and read the Sears catalog, or do other things with it.

Well, I checked the bathroom, and she was not in there reading the catalog, as I had assumed. I only hoped my bladder could take the pain while I waited for this gal to use the bathroom.

Thank God, we got our first lady. Then some more ladies came in.

The Board in New York felt very strongly that the ministry in California should be able to support itself. That was a tough challenge. It seemed that every day we were trying to get enough money to buy food and pay rent.

Believe me, at times I didn't know if we were going to go bankrupt.

Occasionally we would hear about other girls' ministries that had started, but then shut down.

I'd ask why and would be told that they had shut down because they ran out of money.

Even today when people come to me for advice about starting their own girls home and I first talk about the importance of raising enough money. They seem to think this is something trivial, when it is so essential.

Some ministries fail today, not because the staff is not committed, not because there isn't a need, but because there is not enough money.

You have to ask the Holy Spirit to help you devise a plan to make sure finances are available to carry out the ministry.

In Pasadena once, after we got up to eight girls, one day there was a knock on the front door.

I answered it and encountered a man with a stern looking face. He was from the Zoning Board and informed me that I was in violation and could not operate the Home in this part of town.

He asked for my permit. I told him I did not have one. He said it was absolutely necessary for us to appear before the Zoning Board where we could discuss an exemption in order to operate a home in our area.

That made me nervous. In Garrison, I had been through three zoning hearings, and these are some of the toughest experiences I have had in the ministry. You never know how they will turn out.

People you thought were your friends turned out to be your enemies. You cannot believe the things they say against you at a zoning hearing.

We appeared before the City Council for the City of Pasadena with an attorney. Much to our utter disappointment, they turned us down. They said we had to close the Home or would be subject to a massive fine and possible imprisonment.

We sent the ladies from Pasadena to New York, and shut the Home down; however, we were not about to give up.

We rented an apartment for the staff

while we tried to figure this all out. Dispirited, I went to the Pasadena Library and studied the zoning laws.

Through my research, I discovered it was possible to have a home for ladies in any part of California, as long as there were no more than six ladies. I had applied to have eight ladies (that is how many we had at the Home in Pasadena), and they had turned me down.

I made a copy of the zoning law and took it to the Zoning Department in Pasadena. The gentleman looked it over and said, "You're right, Sir. You can have a home for six ladies in any part of the town."

I was really disgusted. Here we had paid this lawyer, had appeared in front of the City Council, and now this.

They could have said, "Okay, you can have six ladies."

But that is not how the system works. The government is always reactionary. They will not tell you what you can do, but they love to tell you what you cannot do. You have to understand that.

So, we began to look for another place.

I got acquainted with some of the people in the zoning department and they told me to look in high-density areas. They said to get out of the one family residential section of the city.

We kept looking and praying. Then, one day I was driving down Cordova Street, turned right on Madison, and there on the left was an older house with a sign on it.

I parked, jumped out of the car, ran up to the front door and knocked. A lady answered. "I'll take it," I said. This shocked her. She kind of stepped backward, smiled, and invited me in.

I took a tour around the house, found it had five bedrooms and three baths. Even though it was old, it would accommodate at least nine ladies.And here is the wonderful part. This woman was a Christian, and her husband worked for World Vision.

They came down on the price, and we were able to make a down payment and purchase the home for $225,000.

Elsie and I managed to rent an apartment across the street. We moved in and soon had nine ladies and a staff. What a miracle!

We lived there for about five years, enjoying the wonderful blessings of the Lord. Yes, we crammed nine ladies in there. We were jammed to the walls. Even though it was crowded with that many ladies in a small house, we somehow survived.

We then found out that the house next door was available for sale.

Again, we were able to scrounge up a down payment and got that one as well. And, lo and behold, we were able to have nineteen ladies at a time.

Three or four years went by. We kept looking for space to expand.

A block and a half away from us sat the Mira Monte Hotel. A low-income hotel that housed drug addicts and you name it.

Suddenly the Mira Monte filed for bankruptcy. We made contact with the courts, hoping to buy it inexpensively through the court system.

There were other organizations that wanted it, but we felt that we would prevail.

However, we were disappointed. A medical doctor bought the hotel. We were very discouraged by that event.

The irony of all this was that every time we passed this hotel on our way back from church, Elsie would say, "Thank you Jesus, for the hotel."

I stayed in constant contact with the bankruptcy court and worked every angle I could, but to no avail. The doctor had locked it up solidly.

I did, however, get acquainted with the doctor. An East Indian, he was a real gentleman. I told him what we did, and he seemed to be interested. I offered to buy the hotel from him.

He said that the price was $1 million, not a dime less. He said he would sell the furnishings for $100,000. I contacted a sympathetic foundation, and they gave us $200,000 for a down payment.

When we moved in, the hotel was really trashed. A drug dealer had lived on the first floor. You can imagine what that apartment looked like, filthy, with rotten food in the refrigerator, holes in the mattresses, holes in the walls, and terribly stained carpeting.

Other rooms were destroyed too. A contractor told us that the electric and plumbing would have to be replaced. But it didn't matter. At least it was a roof over our heads.

Of course, as we found out later, the roof leaked!

We moved in and launched a fund raising campaign, eventually raising $950,000. We still had to get a mortgage on the hotel, plus the renovation was a real challenge. Many churches and other groups adopted rooms, and today we have a beautiful hotel.

In back of the hotel, there was a small two-bedroom cottage. It was trashed as well. This is where Elsie and I planned to live.

The walls were filthy, the carpet stained,

the shower glass broken and nothing seemed to work. It looked horrible. Elsie cried. I felt so sorry for her. I tried to make the best of it. I told her that this was just the beginning.

Elsie is a real homemaker, so we went to work cleaning up the place. Others pitched in and soon the broken down, beat up, old kitchen was replaced by a new one.

Today, this is where Elsie and I still live when we are in California.

It is a nice little home, and very comfortable. In fact, I am writing this book here in my office in that home. As I gaze out my window and admire the hotel, I can't help but reflect on what a great miracle it is.

I have been able to latch onto Elsie's faith, and repeat her hopeful mantra, "Thank you Jesus for the hotel." I find myself saying thank you, a lot.

As Elsie has faith, I have faith, too, for some different things. You, too, can have that faith. Just begin to thank Jesus. If you need some encouragement, just call Elsie, and she will tell you how she got this hotel!

CHAPTER 8

THIS MINISTRY WILL GIVE YOU A NERVOUS BREAKDOWN

I pride myself on the fact that I can take most anything. Except this ministry. You wouldn't believe the enormous amount of pressure it is to handle.

The list is long when trying to help the ladies that society has given up on. These ladies somctimes bring nasty baggage, like the possibility of getting someone killed.

There is the financial responsibility, and the constant pressure that at any moment the telephone could ring, bringing news of disaster. You seem never to escape it.

Even while sitting here writing this book, I am still a bit unsettled over an incident that occurred yesterday. One of the ladies flipped out and was threatening to kill one our staff members and another one of our ladies.

We had to call the police and they took her away in handcuffs. We ask ourselves constantly, "Where else is normal?" It seems there is nothing normal around here.

The personal toll has been tough to handle at times.

At the beginning of this ministry, we had nowhere to go for answers to all of our questions. There was no other girls' home we could turn to and say, "How in the world do you do this?"

We were completely on our own. And because this is "ministry," we gave it all that we had. Certainly, the Call of God was in our lives, and we certainly did not want to shirk from our responsibilities.

That meant very long days with no days off. Who could even think about taking a vacation? That's the way we started.

When we moved to Garrison, Elsie and I lived in the main house with our three children, and all those ladies. Privacy was something that we rarely got, and it began to take its toll.

I'm not really an educated person, and I wasn't prepared for all the administrative challenges this ministry presented. I had to figure it out the best I could, and sometimes I didn't do such a great job. I made plenty of mistakes.

Someone once said that you learn through trial and error. Well I certainly learned a lot. It seemed there were plenty of trials and even more errors!

Looking back, I realize now, we were always learning.

Because of all my responsibilities, I had not yet learned the key management principle of delegating responsibilities. I did everything myself. I even mowed the lawn in Garrison.

At first, the ladies would not wash the dishes because they were scared to death of the dishwasher. It was mechanical and made a lot of noise, so I even had to wash dishes!

During this time, I was also Associate Director for Teen Challenge in Brooklyn. I had to commute five days a week about two hours each way to Brooklyn to carry out my responsibilities there.

On Saturdays, we took the ladies to Saturday Night Services in Brooklyn, so that was another trip.

Sundays were called "rest days," but to me it was more like "passing out day." I was totally exhausted.

Then it caught up with me. I couldn't sleep at night. I knew where I was headed... a nervous breakdown.

I cannot describe to you the feeling you have when this happens. You try to trust in God, but you can't. You try to believe, but you cannot. A force almost satanic in nature drives you, and you cannot control it.

You even try prayer, but that doesn't do any good either. It seems that nothing works.

If any of you have ever had a nervous breakdown, you probably know what I'm talking about.

I was sharing this problem with two of our staff members, Joyce and Shirley. All of a sudden something exploded in my mind. Sitting on the lounge, I burst out crying, and I could not stop.

I knew what I had to do. Kill myself.

The first image that flashed in to my mind was Bear Mountain Bridge. I would jump off and end it all.

I took a deep breath, stood up and said, "I'm getting out of here."

Joyce, who is one of our staff members, saved my life that day.

You have to understand Joyce. She's a very mature Christian woman and is our Business Manager. She's worked for us for twenty-five years, and is one of the steadiest Christians you will ever meet, very consistent.

She's quiet though. Not someone you'd expect any action-packed drama from.

As I stood up, Joyce leaped to her feet, rushed towards me gave a push, knocking me backwards. I stumbled and hit the back of the lounge. Joyce stood towering over me and said, "You're not going anywhere."

I don't know what it was. Maybe it was the shock of seeing Joyce like this. I had never seen her act this way before or since. It really caught me off guard, but it worked. Whatever dark spirit had taken hold of me, Joyce had broken it. I suddenly came to my senses. Joyce and Shirley prayed with me, and I was able to calm down.

Then, I made some decisions. I decided that Elsie and I needed some days off. We needed to take a vacation and (more importantly) turn the ministry over to the Lord.

I used to worry a lot about whether or not we would make it. Among the staff, we came up with a saying, "If we get wiped out, we just start over tomorrow."

Many times we felt like we were going to be wiped out, but we still held on and had faith that we would start all over tomorrow.

One of the wonderful things God has done for me is instill a spirit within that says, "Never give up."

Since that dramatic moment in that room, I have never given up.

I'll be honest, at times when the pressure got unbearable, I felt like giving up.

I'm older now, and I tell myself that an old

man should not be doing this. But then I see some of my contemporaries, older than me, and still in ministry, so I have decided that God provides.

Or, I begin to think that my health is not as good as it used to be. Then, I see other people, caught in a wheel chair, like Joni Erickson, who still carry on. How can I use my tired old body as an excuse?

So, I continue to hang in there and do God's work.

I made some choices that I thought would be best, like readjusting my schedule. That helped for awhile. But then it started to catch up with me again. At first, you make excuses, telling yourself that you have got to do this and you've got to do that.

I'm an avid reader. I've literally read thousands of books. I've always got six or seven books that I am working on. I read a book, I forget the name of it, but the central message was "You've got to re-learn to live."

And that's what I'm doing today. Elsie and I take our days off. We take our vacations. And we have learned to trust God like we have never trusted Him before.

Throughout the years, we have had to monitor our staff carefully for nervous breakdowns. Two of our staff members have suffered nervous breakdowns, and that still hurts to this day. Now we demand that the staff take their days off and take vacations too.

We also have the ladies doing a lot of the ministry that we used to do. Not only is it good management practice, but it allows the ladies the opportunity to assume more responsibility.

In the next chapter, I'll tell you how we have restructured the program to make it more effective.

We have to watch our ladies carefully. Some come to us with mental problems, others have been incarcerated or been in mental institutions. Sometimes these ladies are unable to assume the same daily responsibilities as the other ladies. School, work and other things are at times a great challenge to those with emotional problems.

Melinda was no different.

Melinda is a big girl, about six-foot tall. When she came to us, she fit right into the program and began to study in our school for Christian growth. After a while we noticed a change in her.

We didn't know much about her past, but she admitted that she had a violent temper. She had been in another program and they dismissed her because of her temper. We soon found out that it was more than just her temper.

Melinda began to fall in love with one of our staff members. This relationship was uncomfortable for the staff. We told her to back off.

Instead, she went into a rage that you wouldn't believe and ran towards the kitchen. She grabbed a butcher knife and said that she was going to kill two of our other members, Joyce and Shirley.

I was at the main house when the explosion started. I saw Melinda with a knife. She was screaming for Joyce and Shirley saying she was going to murder them.

The staff snapped into action and hid Joyce and Shirley in another room. Fortunately, there were two locked doors, so she couldn't get through to them. And, she didn't know where they were.

She was ranting and raving and I tried my best to calm her down. Our maintenance man came and tried too, but nothing worked.

Melinda went storming into the kitchen, and I followed her. There was another lady in there as well. I grabbed a nearby stool. Just as I picked it up, the other lady said, "Dad, don't try that."

She took the stool away from me and set it down.

I had planned to hit Melinda in the back of the head and knock her out. It made sense in my desperation, but suppose I didn't knock her out. She could turn on me and murder me with that big kitchen knife.

We quickly called the police but because we were out in the country, it took awhile for them to get there.

When they finally arrived, they encountered Melinda in the middle of the living room. They tried their best to calm her down, but she would have none of it.

She had totally flipped out. The police recognized this. The two cops were kind of whispering among themselves when all of a sudden they lunged towards Melinda and grabbed her knife. They were all rolling on the floor.

I was just standing there when the cop yelled at me, "Reverend, help us out! Help us out!" I jumped into the middle of the fray, we were finally able to pin Melinda down. The police put handcuffs on her and took her away.

I knew what the next step would be. They would commit Melinda to a mental institution. She was out of her mind.

This was a problem though. She could not be committed unless two doctors sanctioned that she was emotionally disturbed.

It is not that easy to commit people to mental institutions. If you falsely commit them, they can turn around, sue the police and any other person involved in committing them, especially in these days of frivolous lawsuits.

I found a doctor. The police took Melinda to him. He saw right away that she was emotionally unbalanced and said, "Yes, commit her."

Then, I tried to find another doctor. That was a tough one. I called a number of doctor friends, and finally I convinced one of them to agree to have her committed. Thank God, he consented.

The police then took her to the mental institution.

Three days later, we got a telegram from the mental institution. Melinda had escaped.

We immediately locked the doors. Believe you me, we were scared. We knew that Melinda would come back, and this time she would kill someone. We waited and waited, but thank God, Melinda never showed up.

Then in the middle of the night, the phone rang. It was Melinda. After her escape, she ended up down in the East Village of New York City. She wanted to talk to me. I spoke to her on the phone and tried my best to help her.

"Dad, what should I do?" Melinda asked.

"You need to go back to the mental institution, Melinda. They can help you there. You need that hospitalization."

"How will I get there?" she asked. "I agree with you, I need to go back, but I am here in New York City and have no money to get there."

After a long pause I said, "I'll come down, pick you up and take you there."

I got out of bed, got dressed, got into my car and went all the way down to New York City to get Melinda. It took about an hour and a half.

She was in a bar. Naturally I kept thinking, "Will she kill me?" But, sometimes you have to live on the edge, and I was going to take a chance.

I got Melinda into the car and we talked about what had happened. I asked her how she had escaped.

"Ah, it was easy," she said. "A tour group was visiting the institution. I just got right in the middle of the group. Can you believe that when they let the tour group out through two secured locked doors, I was still with the group?"

"Once outside the institution, I said 'Good

bye,' to the group. They replied, 'Good bye.'

"They had no idea who I was. Then I got to the road and hitchhiked. A truck driver picked me up, and I ended up here in New York City."

Melinda told me she was willing to go back, so I put her into my car and we headed back up to the mental institution. I knew it would take about two and a half hours to get there even in the middle of the night.

I drove as quickly as I could. About half way, Melinda turned and asked, "Dad, are you afraid of me?"

Somewhere I had learned that in dealing with emotionally disturbed individuals you should never express fear. If you do, something in them will click and they will kill you.

I don't know how many lies I have told in my life, not many. Melinda looked at me. I thought about how it took two cops and me to get her down. If she was going to kill me, I didn't want it to happen now.

I looked Melinda straight in the eye. My heart was pounding in my chest. I took a deep breath and blurted out, "Of course I'm not afraid of you."

I lied.

Now, I am a minister, and lying is one of those things that I try not to make an excuse for, but I did lie. Now don't get me wrong. I have since asked the Lord to forgive me for that lie.

I looked at Melinda, "Just checking to see if you are afraid," she blurted out.

I began to drive faster, breaking the speed limit. Another mistake. Then I looked in the rear view mirror, there were flashing red lights. A cop pulled me over.

I looked over at Melinda. Her head was resting against the window and her eyes were closed. I hoped she was asleep, but I wasn't about to check!

I opened the door and quietly got out. I walked back to the state policeman and said, "Officer, I know you've probably heard a lot of excuses about why people travel fast. I know that you are not going to believe this one, but, I have a lady in my car who's escaped from a mental institution, and I'm taking her back."

He asked me her name and the name of the institution. Next he got on his intercom and called in an inquiry. I heard him talking to someone at the mental institution and sure enough, they verified my story and told him that she had escaped.

We were only about a half hour away from the mental institution. When the word came back confirming that I had an escapee, I figured the policeman would help me. Maybe give me a police escort. Instead, he looked at me and said, "Reverend, It's a nice thing that you're doing. Good luck!" Then he drove away.

I couldn't believe it. Why didn't he help me? To this day, I will never know. I walked back to the car, got in and continued on my mission.

Melinda evidently really was asleep. When I finally got to the mental institution, they were waiting for me. Melinda got out of the car, and it almost seemed like a welcome home party. Everybody there was glad to see her, and Melinda was glad to see them too. I breathed a great sigh of relief, got into my car and headed home.

One week later, we got a telegram. Melinda had escaped again. I expected Melinda to call me from New York City again, but she never did.

About six months later, she did call, but from Baltimore this time.

She was now going to church, serving Christ and living the Christian life. I certainly didn't ask her if she wanted to go back to the mental institution. Melinda and I had a wonderful conversation on the phone. She told me she had learned a great lesson and now she was right with God.

It has been a long time since we have heard from Melinda. I trust all is going well with her. Thank God, that no one was hurt, or even killed, and that the Lord spared us all.

We have to live this scripture; "No person knows what the day may bring forth." It is certainly how we live here at the Walter Hoving Home.

One never knows what to expect. It seems however, that the unexpected always happens here at our home. Thank God, that no matter what happens to us, the Lord continues to take care of us.

As Elsie and I look back on this ministry we have had many heartaches and nearly been killed. Helping these ladies, is an enormous responsibility, yet our testimony is always the same. God has been faithful to us.

I have learned that no matter what we go through, the scripture is still true, "The Lord will deliver us out of all of our troubles."

And, that has happened. Praise the Lord!

CHAPTER 9

RE-ENGINEERING

A number of years ago this guy wrote a book called "*Re-engineering Your Corporation*." Maybe you've heard of it. It was quite popular at the time I read it.

This book really made sense to me. Reading it, I felt the ministry needed some changes. We were doing a pretty good job, but I thought we could do better.

The first change I decided we needed to make was in the dining room. Sitting in the staff section of our dining room one day, I analyzed the layout.

The dining room was divided into two sections; one for the ladies, the other for the staff. The sections were set up differently. The ladies sat in the open room, at unattractive tables, in a section that had linoleum floors. The staff section was further back in the dining room, a private, carpeted area where they sat at nice round tables.

Sitting at a staff table one day, I noticed a

lady standing in between the two sections, right where the linoleum met the carpet. She stood silently looking over at the staff table. How strange, I thought. I leaned over and whispered to one of the staff, "What is the matter with that girl standing there looking at us? Is she emotionally disturbed?"

"Oh, no," she said, "You see, we have a rule here that we, as staff, must have our privacy and the ladies cannot bother us while we are eating. She has to stand there until we acknowledge her."

The staff member continued to eat while that poor little girl just stood there.

I looked at the girl. I looked at the staff. Something happened. A bomb exploded within me. Something was wrong here. This was no way to treat our ladies.

I prayed about it that evening. The following day I came up with a plan.

I told the staff that we were getting rid of all of the round tables in the dining room. Instead, we would have continuous tables. We would then have the wonderful privilege of eating with the ladies.

I said the wrong thing. I almost had a revolution on my hands. The staff (who are wonderful, and I love them!) declared that they did not want to eat with the ladies; they said they had to have their privacy.

All of us have needed our privacy, but not around a dining room table. We were supposed to be a family, and this did not feel like family. I insisted.

We got the long, continuous tables. I asked the staff not to sit together, but to sit with the ladies. Of course, our ladies were excited and felt privileged sitting with the staff. I am not so sure the staff felt the same way. However, everyone adjusted and we learned more about the ladies, and they learned more about us.

Let me tell you about the old ways of doing things.

As I mentioned, when we first started a home for ladies we were strictly on our own. We could not look to any other place for help. Traditionally, the staff held an elevated position within the organization. They were used to barking orders down to the ladies, and there was a great gulf between the staff and the ladies.

As staff, we set up very strict rules. We read all of the ladies incoming mail. We rationalized it saying there might be dope inside the envelope. We monitored their telephone calls. Who knows, they might be making plans for their pimps to come and pick them up, we thought.

In fact, we prided ourselves on the fact that we had twenty-four pages of rules. If a lady disobeyed the rules, she was punished with extra hours of work. The punishment could be anywhere from five hours to a whole Saturday of work depending upon the infraction.

Bless their hearts. We were the dictators, and they better obey us or else.

That kind of structure, however, has its consequences. We were policemen, and the pressure was enormous for some of the staff. I mentioned in an earlier chapter the difficulty we've had with some staff breakdowns.

Well, around this time, two of our staff lost it.

I became more determined to bring change to the ministry. I kept reading more. I went to seminars. I went to management associations, and gradually we began to make changes. The staff had to relinquish some of their power.

That is a difficult thing to do, especially if a person has any type of insecurity. To their credit, the staff was willing to make changes and we embarked on a new adventure.

Another thing we did was have a sign put on the front porch that said, "Welcome to the

Walter Hoving Home."

When a new lady arrived, we put her name on the board, welcoming her. This was often the first time any of our ladies had ever been publicly acknowledged.

In fact, I have even had them stand there and cry.

They could not believe that someone cared that much for them.

In our school for Christian growth, the ladies pass through nine different levels. Within these levels are various subjects that they study and complete. When they have finished with a particular subject, we give them a little certificate with a dot on it.

On Monday mornings, we announce each lady's progress. We have a public display where the ladies place the dots they've earned next to their names, indicating how far along within the nine levels she is.

This way of recognizing the ladies publicly really worked. Sometimes I thought our ladies would even kill to make sure that they earned their dots!

One of the toughest jobs in the ministry is cooking. For instance, how do you like your eggs — scrambled, boiled, fried, not scrambled too much, and fried with butter or what?

I think you know what I mean. Each person has a wide variety of tastes and it is a big chore to satisfy everyone. It is an ongoing problem here at the Home.

Sometimes a lady will go through the line in the kitchen to get her food and forget to be nice. Those poor cooks. They try their best and still they are criticized. To help overcome this problem we started a ritual. While we are still seated in the dining room, the cook comes out of the kitchen after the meal and we all cheer wildly.

With the applause as acknowledgement, the cook is ready to go back into the kitchen and do it again. I have often thought this is what families ought to do. Dad and the kids ought to applaud Mom, rather than criticize the food she cooks. That way, Mom will want to go back into the kitchen knowing that she is appreciated.

Another thing we do is give the ladies a personality profile test. All of us are different. Elsie and I are a good example of that.

I am the type who likes everything in order. I've been given the gift of administration, and everything has to be just right. I am somewhat shy. However, others have observed, even though I am sitting there and not saying anything, I'm still thinking.

Elsie is the opposite. She is outgoing and loves everybody. She can remember names from twenty years ago. She even remembers the clothes someone wore the last time she met them. She easily makes friends. She's absolutely amazing. She has a gift for public relations and it helps our ministry enormously. Whenever we meet important people, or people of wealth, I make sure that Elsie is with me.

At times, well-known people have made contact with this ministry, like Dorothy Carnegie. You have probably heard of Dale Carnegie who wrote the famous book, "*How to Win Friends and Influence People*."

I have actually taken the Dale Carnegie course. I was so overwhelmed by the results that I started teaching some of the principles to the ladies. The principle of how to memorize through the stack method helped me so much that I memorized the whole Sermon on the Mount.

Another thing I learned from the Dale Carnegie course was how to respond when you are given an award. I learned a concept called "**TCUT**." It works like this:**(T)** -When you receive an award you say, **"Thank you." (C)** - You **"credit"** those who made the award possible. **(U)** - You say how you will **"use"** the award. **(T)** - Then, you say **"Thank you"** and sit down.

Ever watch the Oscars, or any of those awards programs on television? The actors and actresses seem to be tongue-tied and sometimes make fools out of themselves. They should learn the **"TCUT"** method.

Anyway, getting back to the story, I got Dorothy Carnegie's address and wrote her a note asking if she would come and speak at the Home. I mentioned that I was using some of the principles from the Dale Carnegie Course to help our ladies get their bearings in life.

Much to my surprise, she called. Yes, she said, she would be more than happy to come and speak to our ladies. I was really excited about that.

The day arrived and Dorothy drove up to our home in a chauffeured limousine. I expected a little old lady with grey hair to slowly emerge from the back seat and hobble up the steps with a cane. Instead, from the back of the limo, a woman with a big bounce to her step appeared. She was wearing a huge smile on her face and lots of make-up. She had a shiny leather outfit on. No one could mistake Dorothy Carnegie for a little old lady!

Dorothy came and spoke at the Home, and that is how we began our acquaintance with her. She then invited Elsie and me to the Dale Carnegie headquarters, where they gave a reception to honor us.

It was mid winter, and we were driving back to Dorothy's after this function.

We hit a snowstorm. Three other people visiting from Japan were with us in the chauffeured limousine. We were all stuck together in the snow on Grand Central Parkway. It didn't look good.

Remember I told you that Elsie and I had been missionaries in Japan? And as I mentioned earlier, Elsie has a way with people. Elsie spontaneously turned to these Japanese people and asked, "Do you want me to sing a Japanese song for you?"

I couldn't believe she asked them that! I thought it was a stupid thing for Elsie to do. Here I was trying to make an impression on Dorothy Carnegie and the others, and Elsie comes out with something like that.

Of course, these people had all taken the Dale Carnegie Course and just nodded "Yes." Elsie began to sing. Was I ever embarrassed!

Finally, when Elsie finished, they applauded. And just like that, Elsie again asked, "Would you like me to sing another song?" True to form, they said, "Yes." Now my face was really getting red.

I could not believe this woman, my wife, with strangers, singing Japanese songs in a chauffeured limousine stalled in the middle of a snowstorm on Grand Central Parkway in New York City.

But that was Elsie.

We finally got moving again. As we approached her place, Dorothy asked Elsie and I to stay overnight. I felt rather uncomfortable with that and said, "I think we can make it home."

We continued through the snowstorm and finally got to our Home in Garrison. Once there, one of the ladies said that Dorothy had called quite concerned about us. Elsie called her back to let her know we had arrived safely.

Through the years, Elsie and Dorothy became very dear friends. We met once a year, and Elsie always remembered what Dorothy wore last year. Elsie was sure to ask about Dorothy's children and grandchildren. Elsie always thinks to ask about things that are really important to the other person.

So help me, I could never remember what Dorothy wore last year. I cannot even remember how many children she has or what has happened to them. But Elsie can, so I let her do the talking . . . and she really makes me look good!

If you are an old timer reading this book, you probably remember Gloria Swanson. She was really into health food long before it became fashionable. I made contact with Gloria and she came up to our Home and spoke on health.

Of course, as you can imagine, Elsie was at her best. Elsie knew how to treat a big star like Gloria Swanson. Gloria soon became a friend of the ministry. In fact, her daughter, also named Gloria, became a member of our board. She is an outstanding Christian woman.

And that brings us back to our ladies. As we learned, each lady is unique, as is each staff member. We accept them the way God made them. I really believe that God gifts each person and we need to accept that. With acceptance of our individual gifts, each person becomes very important in the body of Christ.

We really believe in the potential of our ladies. We purposely do not have many staff members. We, as staff, look upon this ministry as though we are the coaches on the sideline. The ladies help out with the ministry.

When you call the Walter Hoving Home, a lady in the program answers the phone. If you are a new lady coming into the Home, you will be interviewed by one of our ladies. Another lady in the program will be assigned to act as your big sister.

Our ladies advance and can become supervisors. In fact on Saturdays, none of the regular staff is around, as there is a senior lady on duty. I remind her that she acts on behalf of the president, me.

Through the years, we have learned to trust our ladies. Sure, they occasionally make mistakes. Who doesn't? I have certainly made my share, and will continue to do so. However, I am absolutely amazed at the potential of these ladies.

We have unearthed a valuable secret. If you treat the ladies as dignified adults, they will act like adults. If you treat them like children, they will act like children.

Over time, we eliminated many old procedures. We did away with the punishment. Now don't get me wrong, we still maintain a structure. It is not like each lady can do their own little thing; we make it clear that they are part of a large family, with the good of the whole group in mind.

We still have our disciplines and structure. We get up early. We have our daily devotions. We study God's word. We do our duties, and most importantly, we work to become the person that God wants us to become.

Pay telephones were installed so that the

ladies could receive calls, as well as place calls to their own families. We stopped checking their mail.

Oh, sure, occasionally someone will bring in drugs, but the other ladies eventually find out who brought the drugs in, and that lady is disciplined.

We formulated two documents that have become very important to this ministry.

The first lists our values. The second lists the critical success factors that make us what we are today.

The critical success factors are quite long, so I will not mention them here. However, I do want to mention our values. Here they are:

1. We will treat everyone with dignity and respect.
2. We will not complain.
3. We will always be part of the solution, not part of the problem.
4. Our relationships will be guided by I Corinthians 12:12-27. Equal in relationship, different in function.
5. We will support each individual's potential and giftedness.
6. We will give superior service and do every thing with excellence.

As you can see, these values are very important to us.

As I mentioned before, God revealed to me the body of Christ in First Corinthians, twelfth chapter, which states that that we are equal in relationship but different in function. We recognize and respect the differences in each other.

You will notice the part about giftedness. On this issue, we support each other. We want to be a part of each other's future. This means that if someone on the staff decides to move on to some other responsibility, the rest of us support that decision.

Our loss would be someone else's gain. God keeps the records.

I don't want to leave you with the wrong impression. We've hammered and tweaked our system over the years until it works very well, but we still have our share of problems here at the Home.

Sometimes things just don't go right and we do our best to correct them.

Some of our ladies do not mature as fast as we would like them to, and we have problems with that.

Some of our ladies are difficult to trust. We found out the hard way that trust is not something you just give to a person. It is something they must earn.

We have some spare keys at the home,

though we try to keep them to a minimum. Some doors must remain locked. Some people at certain points in their lives simply cannot be trusted, even with the home's automobiles.

Our ladies drive our cars. However, when they first come into the program, we restrict access to the key box for the cars. After a lady has been with us awhile, we see if we can trust her with the cars. If so, then she becomes very important helping us meet the transportation needs of the Home.

Elsie and I fly back and forth between New York and California every other week. A couple of the ladies from the program either take us to the airport or pick us up. We trust them now. Sometimes, unfortunately, it doesn't all work out for the good.

One of our ladies, Melissa, went through the program and stayed on with us. We trusted her with our automobiles. She was helping us out. On one of her days off she took one of the cars and never came back.

We found out later that Melissa went back on drugs and allegedly sold our car to someone else. We waited about three days and then called the police. A couple of days later, the police spotted our car and gave chase.

The girl who bought the car was driving it, high on drugs and driving about ninety miles an hour. It was really dangerous for the cops chasing her. Eventually they caught up to her and apprehended her.

We finally got our car back, and Melissa went to jail for stealing the car and then selling it.

Did that mean that we could no longer trust our ladies with our cars? No.

We have a saying here. When faced with a setback it's called, "The cost of doing business." No matter what system we set up, there will be failures.

Another position we take is that we will never let the few speak for the many.

Occasionally we get letters of criticism. I have these sent to me personally because I want to see if someone has an insight or valid criticism. Sometimes they do and we make corrections and/or apologies.

The girl, Melissa, who stole our car, asked for our help after she got out of jail. A most unusual case, she had actually stayed at our home five different times. We had decided after the car incident never to take her back again.

We couldn't believe it when she called from jail and wanted help again. But something moved in my heart. As I look back now I realize that it was the Holy Spirit. I said,

"Yes, come on back again."

The rest of the staff really was not pleased. I tried to explain to them that it was the will of the Lord to let Melissa back. And so she returned.

This time it worked. Today Melissa is married. She adopted a little boy, and she and her husband are outstanding Christians in their church. Melissa has been saved for about ten years, now.

It just goes to prove that you never really have all of the answers.

I will say that the ministry today is better off than it ever has been. However, I still feel that we have a long way to go.

There are always more ladies out there who need our help. We still have to take risks. I don't have all the answers. In fact, sometimes I feel like I do not really have any answers, but I keep plodding along.

Thank God for all of the ladies who succeed. They come out with a strength unknown to most Christians, and some of our ladies now even have their own ministries.

Thank God, for all of those who are serving the Lord . . . in spite of our many mistakes.

CHAPTER 10

Staying Clean

Sometimes I'm asked, "John, do you ever get tempted by the ladies in the program?"

I mentioned before that I was a red blooded American man, and, of course, I get tempted.

Some people think that we ministers have no feelings whatsoever. But if we're really honest with ourselves, we have to admit, of course, we're tempted.

You must understand that many of these ladies are former prostitutes. Having spent a lifetime turning guys on, when they come here to the Home, that lifestyle is still a part of them.

It reminds me of a story that you may know. Remember years ago when President Jimmy Carter was running for president? He did an interview with Playboy Magazine. The writer asked President Carter if he was ever tempted. Bless his heart, Jimmy Carter was honest. He said that occasionally he had some thoughts of lust.

The story did not end there. Around the same time, the writer of the article happened to ask a nationally known evangelist the same question, and this evangelist said, no, he never had thoughts of lust. I honestly question that.

Sometime later, Jimmy Carter became president. This same evangelist wrote President Carter and asked if the President would come to his college and speak.

President Carter wrote back and said that he was too sinful to speak at this school. I really liked President Carter's tongue and cheek reply since, Jimmy Carter had admitted his lust and this preacher had not.

Elsie and I have been married since 1952 and have enjoyed many wonderful years together. Prior to getting married, we had a wonderful courtship. Not without problems though.

If you have ever met Elsie, you know what an absolutely fantastic gal she is; outgoing, great personality, loves everybody, and she is very passionate. When we were courting and would go out parking in my car, Elsie was so passionate that she steamed up my windows so badly that I could hardly see to drive! (Just kidding — though I don't think my windows got steamed up from an overheated radiator!)

Elsie and I were tempted to have sex before marriage. If you actually think about it, it is only natural. God gave us those innate instincts to make sure that the human race would propagate. However, thank God, we did not fall into that temptation.

Years later when our children began dating, Elsie and I had the wonderful privilege of explaining to them the benefits of resisting sexual temptation.

This ministry does have its humorous stories about sexual temptations, as well as some serious ones. Let me tell you a humorous one.

Bob Combs, a graduate of Boston University, was doing his masters degree on photography. He decided to make a photo journal about the ministry of Teen Challenge and to include the women of The Walter Hoving Home.

Bob came to us and said he needed to get some pictures of prostitutes on the street.

One afternoon I took him in my car, and we went up to 110th and Madison Avenue in New York City. We pulled up to the curb, and I saw three girls leaning against a building who were evidently prostituting.

I told Bob to roll down his window. One of the girls came over and walked right up to the car. She was kind of bold and actually stuck her whole head in the window, right in front of Bob.

Now, you have to know Bob. He is from Ithaca, New York, from a country church and very, very shy. At that time, he wasn't married, just a single guy.

This young lady looked at me and then looked at Bob and said, "Want to have a good time?" It's the question they always ask. I looked over at Bob. He actually was shaking, red as a beet. I started to laugh.

The lady looked at me and said, "What's the matter? Are you guys cops?"

"I'm a minister," I replied.

She laughed. "Okay, then, preacher. You can have it free."

Bob's mouth dropped open. I laughed some more, and then told the gal that there was more in life than prostitution and drugs. We told her about Jesus.

It was great working with Bob. He also needed to take pictures of a girl actually shooting drugs.

Elsie and I had gotten to know Mickey, a big drug dealer up in the Bronx. She was the kind of dealer who was also a drug addict.

Mickey was a beautiful girl who had come into our home to kick "cold turkey." Twice she came, but she couldn't take the kicking.

We encountered another girl, Vivian, from the Bronx who was kicking her habit cold turkey. She was really, really sick and couldn't take it. She pled with us to take her back to the Bronx. Because she was in so much pain, Elsie and I agreed. She could not take the train in her condition, so Elsie and I loaded her into our car.

Kicking cold turkey has a lot of physical problems. There is a lot of diarrhea and vomiting. We took along a bedpan. Heading down to the Bronx, poor little Vivian was in the back seat throwing up, and filling the bedpan from the other end. We had to stop a couple of times to empty the bedpan.

It was not a very pleasant experience, but sometimes in this ministry, these are the types of things you have to do.

When we got to the Bronx, Vivian led us to Mickey's apartment. These drug dealers are smart. They have people stationed outside to warn them of police. We had to pass through people standing on the street, as well as in front of Mickey's apartment. Finally, we were inside and told Mickey about Vivian's situation.

Mickey saw Vivian suffering and gave her some dope and a needle. Vivian went into the bedroom and took drugs while we were there. It was supposed to be just enough to help her detox slowly.

Then Vivian came out of the bedroom and passed out. She had overdosed. I watched Mickey. She immediately blew air into Vivian's lungs.

Standing there, watching this happen, I was scared to death. Suppose she did die? Suppose the police came? What would we say?

Believe me, it was an awkward situation. Finally, thank God, — and I was really praying — Vivian regained consciousness and got up.

Elsie and I left Mickey's place. Unfortunately, Vivian didn't come back with us. Thank God, years later we did hear from her and today she is doing well —completely free from drugs.

Anyway, back to the story of Bob Combs.

Since Bob wanted a picture of a girl getting high, I thought I would go over to Mickey's and see if she could arrange it for us.

We went to Mickey's. Of course, we had to go through the two guys standing watch outside of the building and then up the stairs where some other guys were guarding the place. Finally, we were inside Mickey's apartment.

Mickey trusted me. She knew that I wouldn't bring a cop in, even though Bob could have passed for one.

Because we are out on the streets so much, Elsie and I see all sorts of things. We see drug deals constantly. We know who the drug addicts are and who the pushers are.

Sometimes people say, "Well, why don't you call the cops on them?"

If the addicts on the streets thought that we would call the cops, that would have been the end of our ministry. Of course, there was also the possibility of being shot the next time we come back if they thought we were turning them in to the police.

I hope you understand this. I certainly do not condone drug addiction or the sale of drugs, but sometimes you have to be street-wise. I have found out that no matter what we see, we never want to compromise our relationship with those addicts on the streets who really need to know the Lord.

The addicts trust us. Same with the dope dealers. Sometimes when we are on the streets and there is talk of a killing, some of these addicts and pushers come to us and say, "Reverend, it's going to come down in a minute or two, you'd better get out of here now."

They know when a shooting is about to

take place and they look out for our safety. Immediately, I get into the car and leave. So far, thank God, I'm still alive.

So, anyhow, Bob and I went up to Mickey's apartment. She was so happy to see me. We hugged and again I felt so helpless about how to help this wonderful gal really come to a saving knowledge of Christ. She is such a dear friend to Elsie and me.

I told Mickey about Bob and the photo journal that he was doing. I said that we were looking for a lady who was going to shoot drugs. Much to my surprise Mickey said, "I'm going to get off. You can take pictures of me."

Right there in that apartment Bob took the pictures. He got pictures of the whole procedure a drug addict goes through; from opening the bag of heroin, to putting it in a bottle cap, heating it up and drawing the liquid heroin into the syringe. Then the moment came when Mickey had to inject herself.

Mickey had had a long run with heroin and most of the veins in her arms and legs had collapsed. There was only one place where she could get a hit and that was in her hip.

Mickey looked at me and said, "Dad B, I don't want to embarrass you, but I have to raise my skirt to get a hit." I said, "I understand."

Mickey raised her dress and plunged the

needle into her hip. When an addict pushes the end of the syringe, they do it slowly. They want to make sure that it gets into the bloodstream.

Bob was taking pictures like crazy. All of a sudden he yelled out, "Nuts! I ran out of film!" Mickey looked up to Bob and said, "I'll just wait for you to reload your camera."

Mickey sat there with a needle hanging in her hip, Bob reloaded his camera and took some more pictures. We finished and got ready to leave. I went to tell Mickey goodbye.

I hugged Mickey, not knowing that tragically, this would be the last time I would see Mickey alive. I hug a lot of ladies as a father would hug a daughter. We thanked Mickey and left. A number of months later, I heard that Mickey died from a drug overdose.

Even today, that really grieves my heart. Mickey was such a beautiful young lady with great potential, a wonderful person. Unfortunately, she was bound in the trap of addiction, and it killed her.

Sometimes I have the gift of discernment. Not often, but sometimes the Holy Spirit will speak to my heart and I am able to discern things.

Through the years, we have had many unmarried staff members. Never had any of the staff crossed the line between them and me except this one time.

I had gone into the staff's office on business and there she was sitting on her desk. She had been divorced before and I am sure was looking for another man — which is okay, but you have to be careful about who that man is.

As she sat at her desk, we looked over some papers. I walked up to her and bent over, looking down at the papers. After talking a few moments, I felt her hand on my back. She started rubbing my back and then dropped her hands lower.

I looked at her. She had a big smile on her face. I felt so stupid. I'd been around the block a few times myself. I knew what she wanted.

I consider myself a kind person, but you have to be careful how far your kindness goes. As soon as she dropped her hands lower on my back I just ignored her, moved to the other side of her desk and continued the conversation.

Elsie and I have a rule. If a girl makes a pass at me, I immediately tell Elsie. This does two things.

Number one, Elsie will keep her eye on that girl and make sure that the girl and I will not be alone together.

Two, since Elsie knows what is going on, there's no thrill of the chase.

I let Elsie know about this staff member, and we prayed about it. About three months later, this staff member decided to resign and leave. God took care of the problem.

But we have had other problems.

We had a wonderful staff member, Bernice, who was married. Her husband, Ernie, was on staff at the Brooklyn Teen Challenge. We let Bernice live in the city to be with her husband and commute up to Garrison to participate in our educational program.

Sometimes Bernice's husband would come up to Garrison with her. He seemed like a nice guy to have around.

We'd recently gotten another couple into the program, Marcie and Phil. Phil went to Teen Challenge, where Bernice's husband worked. Marcie, his wife, came to Garrison. When Ernie was in Garrison, he would let Marcie know how her husband was doing in Brooklyn.

Marcie was working in the kitchen one day when I walked in for something. I saw Ernie and Marcie talking. I assumed that Ernie was letting Marcie know how her husband was doing.

That evening, after Ernie and Bernice left to go back to their apartment in the city, Marcie came to us and said, "Ernie propositioned me. He wanted to take me down to the basement and into the bathroom to have sex with me. He thought that because I don't live with my husband all of the time that I needed sex."

The following day I had to go down to the Brooklyn Teen Challenge. I saw Ernie. I called him into my office and told him what Marcie had said. Ernie looked at me with a sad face and said, "I'm really shocked and hurt that you would even think that I would say something like that. I would never, never under any circumstance do anything like that."

I was embarrassed to think that I had accused Ernie of something like that. It was something I was sorry for. I apologized to Ernie.

When I returned to the Home that night, we dismissed Marcie for lying to us. She called her husband and he too left the program. I've not seen them since. But, the story does not end there.

I was still Associate Director of Brooklyn Teen Challenge and commuted between Garrison and New York City.

I prayed a lot about this problem and the Holy Spirit kept telling me that Ernie really did proposition Marcie. I really struggled with that.

Was the Holy Spirit really speaking? Or was it just my mind speaking? I wrestled and wrestled with that one.

I kept praying, but the thing would not come out of my spirit. So, I thought I would talk to Ernie again. I called him into my office.

This time Ernie was really angry. He sat there and suddenly jumped to his feet and yelled at me, "Dad B, I just can't believe this! I would never, never do anything like that!" He stomped out of my office. I sat there really embarrassed. For sure, I was going to forget about it and go on my way.

A couple of weeks later I went back to the Brooklyn Teen Challenge. I walked by the chapel. Ernie was up at the pulpit preaching. He was preaching like a house on fire.

My first thought was that if he preached like that he must be innocent of the accusation. But my inner voice spoke loud and clear. It almost seemed to shout, "Ernie is guilty!"

God had spoken again. I talked back to the Lord. I even questioned the Lord. I just could not get it out of my spirit. So help me, I thought it was over. But then I knew that when you really think about these things, it is the still small voice that speaks.

You know that voice is God.

Later that afternoon I called Ernie into my

office. I apologized for calling him back for the third time. I told him that as I walked by the chapel the Holy Spirit had spoken to me again.

Then I said, "Ernie, I'm going to ask you this once again, and you'd better tell the truth. You are not talking to me; you are talking to the Holy Spirit. If you lie to the Holy Spirit, some tragic thing will happen to you just like it happened to Ananias and Sapphira in the Book of Acts. The Lord killed them. Do you understand me?"

Ernie had his head down. "Ernie, did you proposition Marcie?" I asked. There was a long pause, then Ernie slowly raised his head, "Yes, I did."

I started to weep. I knew what this would mean to the relationship between Ernie and his wife, Bernice.

This story has a tragic ending. Ernie resigned as a staff member. Later on he backslid and died. I have found out that it pays to stay clean. Tragic things happen to those who have not learned to say no to temptation.

I am not above temptation. It comes up and I still have to deal with it. Some people join accountability groups to keep them straight.

I think that's wonderful. But I'm really not that type of person. For me, my "accountability group" is when I meet the Lord every morning of every single day, during my devotional time, when I am transparent before the Lord.

I have to confess my temptations, lay them on the table, and then go on with life. That is what works for me. Others may need accountability groups.

A few years ago, I heard about a very well known author and pastor of a huge church. He was a strong advocate of accountability groups and participated in them. Later it turned out that the whole time he had been attending accountability groups, he had been having illicit sexual relations with his secretary. When he was found out, he had to leave the ministry.

Evidently, this pastor did not have a strong link with the Lord on a daily basis.

In my case, because of my personal devotions, I do not find the need for an accountability group, but you may need one. Just ask the Holy Spirit how you should be held accountable.

Terrible consequences await those who have fallen into immorality. Some of our best -known Christian public figures have lost their ministry and their effectiveness because of moral failure.

This problem is now more prevalent than ever. But, thank God, Elsie and I have many friends who pray for us. I do not want my life to end up in the wreckage of immoral failure.

I constantly pray, "God, keep me clean."

I hope that's your prayer, too.

CHAPTER 11

Is It Really Worth It?

This ministry has really taken a toll on my life. If it isn't one thing, it's another.

As I mentioned previously, sometimes my life is in jeopardy. This can be because someone is trying to physically kill me, or because they are trying to ruin my reputation with accusations of sexual improprieties.

As you have learned, we now have two Walter Hoving Homes, one in New York and one in California. Elsie and I are in charge of both of them. That means one week in New York, one week in California, one week in New York, one week in California throughout the year.

Let me tell you, we have never gotten used to jets — it's like getting a dose of the flu once a week — but we still struggle aboard the airplane and do God's work the best we can.

Our finances are never secure. We never have enough money to support this ministry. We are living on the edge most of the time.

With no endowment to rely on, we just trust in the Lord.

And problems always arise with the ladies. You name the problem, and we've been there. You think you have a problem with your wife, mother or sister? How would you like to have a whole group of women like that? Just multiply the problems you might expect to have.

It can get tough at times. This past year has been one of the toughest financially. We have been on the brink of bankruptcy twice.

People talk about sleepless nights. I have sleepless years!

And then, there are the neighbors. It is hard to believe, but at times, they do not like us.

I mean, they really do not like us.

Like the zoning hearings.

As I mentioned previously, we have been through four zoning hearings. They are knock down, drag out affairs that pit friends against friends, eventually turning them into enemies.

I do not like them at all. But, it's part of the laws of our communities and we must live by them. Neighbors have the right to protest if something is happening that they do not feel comfortable with.

The first zoning hearing we had in Garrison was one of the worst. The lies that the neighbors told about us were absolutely unbelievable!

They accused us of selling drugs out of our home, and other outrageous things like setting up a roadside booth to sell marijuana. In fact, one neighbor was so afraid that he went and bought a gun because he thought that our ladies might rob his house.

We won the first zoning hearing, three to two. Thank God, the chairman of the zoning board was a woman who had heard about us at a reception at the Osborn Castle in Garrison when we first moved there.

In Garrison when you look out our window, you can see on the mountainside a beautiful castle. That's the Osborn Castle. The Osborns and the Hovings were close friends. In fact, General Osborn and Walter Hoving started the U.S.O.

When we moved up to Garrison, the Osborns thought it would be a good idea to have a reception for us at their castle. They invited some of the leading people of this very wealthy community. There are a number of estates around here, and many people knew the Hovings through Tiffany's.

I attended the reception, along with two of our ladies who came to give their testimonies. The guests, of course, were not a totally Christian group. They were having their cocktails, and we were there to share with them the Gospel of Christ.

Before the meeting, Mrs. Hoving came up to me and said, "John, remember that this is a mixed group. Be careful what you say."

I knew what she meant. I wasn't supposed to tell these people about Jesus.

We got up and spoke about the Home. Our two ladies testified. Bless those dear ladies. They really shared the gospel about how Jesus dramatically changed their lives. That was years ago, and today both of those ladies are outstanding Christians.

After I spoke, some of the guests asked for a question and answer period. About fifty people were there. As I stood before the group, some of them sat there staring at me while smoking their cigarettes. Mr. and Mrs. Hoving were in the front row.

The first question that was asked was "How is your program different than other programs?"

I paused, considering my answer, when Mr. Hoving jumped up, turned to face the group and loudly proclaimed, "The difference between our program and other programs is Jesus."

I guess Mrs. Hoving had not talked to him

about this mixed group. Walter Hoving didn't care. As I would later learn, he always took a very strong stand for Jesus.

But, as the Holy Spirit would have it, in the audience that night was the chairman of the zoning board. I did not know who she was at the time, but later on, I found out. She was the member of the zoning board who ended up casting her vote in favor of us staying in Garrison.

We decided to expand. Another zoning hearing was scheduled. Once again, there was heavy opposition, and they were well organized this time. For sure they were not going to let us expand.

It looked as if expansion here would not be possible. Maybe we should sell the place and move somewhere else. I went down to see Mr. Hoving at Tiffany's and told him that we might have to sell the place.

I will never forget Mr. Hoving's response. When I said, "We might have to move," he said, "John, you can't do that. Jesus is in the walls up there."

Well, thank God, we made it through that zoning hearing.

One of our neighbors who led the opposition was a retired lawyer. He got the people all worked up, and hundreds came to that zoning hearing. Still, we prevailed and won that one too.

It is true that the presence of Christ is here at the homes.

The lawyer who had opposed us at that hearing later had a heart attack. I heard about it and went down to the hospital to pray for him. He could not believe it that I would come to see him.

After he got out of the hospital, we kept in contact with he and his wife, and visited them quite often.

A few years later we had another zoning hearing.

This retired lawyer who had opposed us the first two times, was now our friend. He said whatever we wanted to do at the Home was okay with him. We had not only gained a friend, but an ally as well.

The neighbors at the end of the driveway hated us. I tried to make friends with them.

One day the man was out in the yard with his two little children and I stopped by.

We had quite a bit of acreage and occasionally kept a horse for the ladies, but at this particular time, the barn was empty. I told the man that our barn was empty and if he wanted to get a horse for the kids, he could use our barn and corral free of charge.

"Reverend, I don't want a horse. Okay?" he snarled.

So much for friendly neighbors.

Six months later we heard these neighbors were moving. I knew that God had answered my prayer. He was helping me get rid of those mean, ornery people.

We rejoiced when they moved. Thank God, the neighbors who replaced them were not mean. But would you believe it? A year later the mean neighbors decided to move back.

I kept examining my life. I must have sinned to cause this to happen. I am not that righteous. I could think of a few things that I might have done. Still, I just could not believe this was happening to us again.

I prayed about the inevitable upcoming disaster when these ornery neighbors moved back, and the Lord really spoke to me.

The Lord said, I was to welcome them with a cake that said, "Welcome back!"

I could not believe what the Lord was saying to me! I didn't want to welcome these people back. As far as I was concerned, I wished they would drop dead and never come back.

But I did as the Lord told me to.

I got the ladies to bake a cake, and sure enough, we put "Welcome back" on it. When we delivered it, the mean neighbors were so shocked, they almost passed out. They probably thought the cake was poisoned.

I heard later that they enjoyed the cake very much. And this time around, they were friendly. I guess the cake did it.

Later, they were ready to move again. The husband was an electrician and moved around the country quite a bit. He and his wife heard that we needed to expand and were looking for some more room.

They asked if we would be interested in renting their house. And we did. We ended up having a wonderful relationship with these neighbors. They are very dear people. It's amazing what God can do.

To answer the question posed at the beginning of this chapter, "Is it really, really worth it?" I can say, yes, it is.

Even though Elsie and I have gone through some very deep waters and put our lives on the line many times, I would do it all over again. My only regret is that I did not begin the ministry sooner.

It has been worth it.

The rewards and results of this ministry are absolutely unbelievable.

Like the story of Monica. Monica was a drug addict and actually behaved like a wild animal. She would get high, run off into the streets in her pajamas and leave her two children behind, uncared for. The neighbors were scared to death of her.

Some of her neighbors had heard about the Walter Hoving Home and sent Monica to us. When she arrived, she was beyond description.

She did not have much education; was really weird, and right on the edge of being insane.

But we accepted her. As Monica progressed through the program, the Lord not only saved her and filled her with the Spirit, but she became a woman of prayer.

And we loved her two little girls.

The kids' weekend is the greatest thing! These little kiddies are so happy to see their mothers. The Lord begins to reunite them. We teach parenting courses to help the mothers. It is so rewarding to see the ladies accept their responsibility as mothers when we get them together with their kids.

When Monica's little girl, Janice, was about three years old, I was sitting in the office one day and she came running up to me with a piece of paper in her hand. I looked down at her. She had a big smile on her face.

Her two little hands reached up handing

me this piece of paper. She mumbled something incoherent in her shy little voice.

I took the paper and said, "Janice, is this for Grandpa?"

Elsie and I are Mom and Dad to the ladies, Grandma and Grandpa to their children.

Janice nodded her little head. Then she lifted her sweet arms up to hug me. As I reached down to pick her up I shall never forget those little arms wrapped around my neck, squeezing me tightly.

As I returned her hug I thought, it is because of our ministry that this darling little girl's mother has been saved. Now Janice's mom can be a real mother to her, no longer the woman she was, so consumed by her demons that she could not care for her child.

Writing this book, I think back upon that day. I have to stop and gain my composure as I sit here weeping over the restoring power of Jesus, able to bring children and mothers back together again.

A number of years have gone by since then. Today Monica is the director of a Christian rehabilitation center for men and women. Her two little daughters are beautiful, Christian young ladies.

Is it worth it? Yep, it sure is.

Today, there are so many of our graduates

living virtuous Christian lives. Other ladies like Monica run other girls' homes. Some are missionaries. Some are pastor's wives.

Some have gone on to get their doctorate degrees and are great Christian educators. Others have become very wealthy. Many have returned to society to live life as any normal woman or mother would.

Some people ask Elsie and I when we plan to retire. Our reply is always the same. We will keep going as long as our health holds out, or until Jesus comes to take us home.

Yes, we continue to face the most trying circumstances and confront a difficult battle. But in the end, because of Jesus, we always come out victorious.

I hope this information about our home is of interest to you. As mentioned earlier, we are an open ministry and welcome visitors. It is because of the prayers and gifts of people like you that we continue to keep our doors open.

Elsie and I hope one day to personally meet you, if we have not already done so.

Thanks again for your prayers and gifts, and for what the Lord is doing at both of the Walter Hoving Homes.

Since 1967, thousands of young women have found new life and new hope at the Walter Hoving Home. The Walter Hoving Home is nationally recognized for the high cure rate among the alcoholic and drug addicted women who complete its spiritually-oriented rehabilitation program. Here, they have found a happy, healthy way of living through the power of Christ. The success of the program is made possible through the prayers and support of individuals who are committed to helping young ladies gain freedom from the bondage of drugs, alcohol and prostitution.

Will you help us in this work by sending a gift today?

Walter Hoving Home
P. O. Box 194
Garrison, New York 10524
845-424-3674

... or

Walter Hoving Home
P. O. Box 94304
Pasadena, California 91109
626-405-0950

YOUR GIFT WILL HELP EACH LADY GET THE CHANCE SHE DESERVES.

The Walter Hoving Home depends upon the contributions of friends like you to help cover the costs of caring for the hundreds of young women who come to the facility in New York and California. At our residential rehabilitation program, we provide food, shelter, clothing, medical care, educational and vocational training as well as spiritual guidance and Christian teaching. If you can please send a gift to help an abused and neglected lady find new life.

YES! I will help you rescue young ladies through the Walter Hoving Home. I'm enclosing my gift of:

❑ $15 ❑ $50 ❑ $100 Other ________

____
NAME

____
ADDRESS

____
CITY STATE ZIP

Please make your check payable to the **Walter Hoving Home**. *Your gift is tax deductible.*

Walter Hoving Home
127 So. El Molino
P.O. Box 94304, Pasadena, CA 91109 ... or

Walter Hoving Home
Avery Road
P. O. Box 194, Garrison, NY 10524

CUT HERE AND MAIL IN